PASTORAL ANSWERS

PAST⊕RAL
ANSWERS

M. Francis Mannion

OUR SUNDAY VISITOR PUBLISHING DIVISION
OUR SUNDAY VISITOR, INC.
HUNTINGTON, INDIANA 46750

Dedicated to Mrs. Arlita Llenares,
who faithfully typed
my "Pastoral Answers" column
for *Our Sunday Visitor* newspaper
over the years and served
as wise counselor on their contents.

CONTENTS

INTRODUCTION

If theology is "faith seeking understanding," as St. Anselm defined it, then all believers could be considered "theologians" in a limited sense. By opening ourselves even slightly to the precious gift of faith, we will inevitably ponder questions about what we believe as we struggle to grasp more clearly the mysteries we so faintly perceive. The very act of picking up this book and flipping through its pages — whether undertaken out of sincere interest in the subject matter at hand or mere curiosity — is symptomatic of a yearning for answers and explanations regarding faith and its practice.

Our search for meaning and understanding entails not only the "big questions" — such as the attributes of God, the means of salvation, and the end of the world — but also relatively smaller issues of Church structure, Scripture passages, liturgical norms, prayer and spirituality, or everyday morals and ethics. One frequently wonders: What does the Church teach on this or that subject? Where did this or that practice originate, and is it of sound Catholic pedigree? Where do I find that teaching in Scripture, or in the *Catechism of the Catholic Church*? And, assuming I do succeed in finding it, who can tell me what it all means for me here, now, as I struggle to live, pray, and serve God in my rather ordinary life?

That's where Msgr. M. Francis Mannion steps in.

Msgr. Mannion, director of The Liturgical Institute at Mundelein Seminary/University of Saint Mary of the Lake near Chicago and former longtime rector of the Cathedral of the Madeleine in Salt Lake City, Utah, knows how to express official Church teaching in ordinary language, and how to apply the Church's wisdom in common situations. He's been doing just that through his very popular column, "Pastoral Answers," which has appeared in *Our Sunday Visitor* newspaper every week since its debut in the spring of 1997. He's one of the leading Catholic "answer men" in the United States today. What sets him apart, though, is how he puts his own signature on the craft — and with delightful results.

Sure, he'll give you the pertinent Church teaching or scriptural reference, and he'll even cite line and verse. The necessary documentation is always there.

But he's more than a theological concordance for Catholics. His responses are peppered with a seasoning of "Mannionisms" — a tasty mix of subtle humor, Irish wit, self-deprecating references, and ironic caricatures that helps make "Pastoral Answers" perhaps the best-read weekly Catholic Q&A column in print.

What's more — and true to the title of his column and this book — Msgr. Mannion offers that loving pastor's touch as he seeks to guide the reader ever so gently into authentic worship, moral and ethical clarity, and an awareness of the immense truth and beauty present in the rich teachings and traditions of the Catholic faith.

He might not satisfy the knee-jerk conservative Catholic who seeks a caustic, self-righteous tongue-lashing on all liberal or "progressive" Catholics, nor will he endear himself to those who wish to fashion the Church's moral and social teachings or liturgical practices to suit their own limited vision. Instead, with a wry smile and a sharp intellect, he both educates and counsels the inquisitive soul with concise, straight answers. Pastoral answers.

Here are crisp responses to a mix of queries both profound and mundane, offered by an experienced parish priest and eminent theologian who remains ever mindful that, after all, it's people's souls that are ultimately at stake.

For the theologian in all of us, the search for understanding has never been so much fun.

— Gerald Korson
Editor, *Our Sunday Visitor*

ONE

Catholic Belief and Doctrine

Church
God
Catechism
Creed
Salvation
Last Things
Mary
Heresy
Oddities

One True Church

Question: *I am confused as to how to understand non-Catholic churches. Before Vatican II, Catholicism claimed to be the one true church. Now do we believe that all churches are equal?*

Answer: On this matter, you could not do better than read both the Constitution on the Church and the Decree on Ecumenism of Vatican II. The Constitution on the Church states that there is one church of Christ and that this church "subsists" in the Catholic Church (no. 8). The word "subsists" is entirely consistent with traditional claims that the Catholic Church is "the one true" Church of Christ.

The word "subsists," however, also allows Catholicism to regard other Christian churches positively. The Decree on Ecumenism provides the key principle here when it states: "Some, even very many, of the most significant elements and endowments which together go to build up and give life to the Church itself, can exist outside the visible boundaries of the Catholic Church: the written Word of God; the life of grace; faith, hope and charity, with the other interior gifts of the Holy Spirit, as well as visible elements." Accordingly, "the separated Churches and communities as such, though we believe they suffer from [some] defects," have been "by no means deprived of significance and importance in the mystery of salvation." In varying degrees, the liturgical life of each church or community "can truly engender a life of grace" and "can aptly give access to the communion of salvation" (no. 3).

When pressed, even more liberal Catholics do not believe that all churches are equal (The Aaronic Church of White Supremacy is equal to the Greek Orthodox Church? Hardly!). Vatican II provides the means by which it is possible to hold that the Catholic Church is the one true Church of Christ, while regarding other Christian communities positively.

Catholic Evangelism

Question: *A Protestant evangelist recently said on local television that the Catholic Church does not evangelize. Why is it that we Catholics are not more aggressive in promoting the faith?*

Answer: Aggressiveness in the promotion of faith is, in my judgment, no virtue. Among the historic expressions of this style of "evangelism" have been inquisitions and holy wars — traditions for which we should feel no nostalgia!

Today aggressiveness more generally takes the form of proselytism: the use of mental or spiritual coercion to overwhelm the non-member into an acceptance of the promoter's faith. Proselytism is generally associated with fundamentalist groups and new religious movements. The Catholic Church rejects proselytism and shies away from the kind of aggressive "talking" evangelism today found on television and in door-to-door missionary programs.

Authentic evangelization should be distinguished from proselytism. Genuine evangelization is the proclamation of the Gospel in a manner that demonstrates the inner attractiveness of the Christian life. The human dignity and conscience of the one encountering the Gospel, either for the first time or in a deeper way, is fully respected. He or she is brought to faith not by coercion but by the intrinsic power of Christian belief and witness.

Catholic evangelism occurs through the power of the liturgy well celebrated, men and women being catechized to live out their faith well, the poor being served, clergy and people promoting the common good. When Catholic parishes, hospitals, charitable organizations, colleges, and universities do their job well, the Gospel is being effectively proclaimed. The Catholic Church in the U.S. has, in this regard, an exceptional evangelical history.

Someone once said: "The Christian is required to proclaim the Gospel by every means possible, and, if necessary, use words." Sound advice!

The Unknowable God

Question: *This prayer was recently printed in our parish bulletin: "Great Unknowable God, you are the wind and the silence, the darkness and the light; you are simplicity and paradox. Draw us into your mystery! Teach us the language of symbol and simile; sing for us the melody of metaphor. Unite us in the communion of ritual, that in our worship we may be transformed by your love. We ask this in your name, God-beyond-naming, who lives and reigns forever and ever. Amen." I am very uncomfortable with the prayer. Please comment on it.*

Answer: It must have been a slow bulletin week in your parish! There are two things wrong with this prayer. First, it calls God "unknowable," a "God-beyond-naming." That's fine if you're a Unitarian, but not if you are a traditional Christian. Consider Matthew 11:27: "No one knows the Father except the Son and anyone to whom the Son chooses to reveal him." Jesus revealed God as Father, giving us the "Our Father" as our privileged mode of intercession. God in the Christian tradition is certainly not "unknowable" or "beyond-naming," even as God always escapes complete human comprehension.

Second, the prayer is highly abstract. It might work in a feminist-leaning university community (a likely origin of material of this sort), but is apt to draw a blank if ever used in a church full of average Catholics. A prayer that combines words like "paradox," "simile" and "metaphor" is not likely to cut it after a depressing day at work or when you're worried sick about your ailing mother.

God as Mother

Question: *I am not a feminist, but I wonder if it is ever right to think of God as "mother."*

Answer: Certainly, it is. No less an authority than Pope John Paul II says so. In his 1988 Apostolic Letter "On the Dignity and Vocation of Women," the pope points to biblical passages that attribute feminine qualities to God.

Pope John Paul writes: "We may quote here some characteristic passages from the prophet Isaiah: 'But Zion said, "The Lord has forsaken me, my Lord has forgotten me." "Can a woman forget her sucking child, that she should have no compassion on the son of her womb? Even these may forget, yet I will not forget you" ' (49:14-15). And elsewhere: 'As one whom his mother comforts, so will I comfort you; you shall be comforted in Jerusalem' (66:13). In the Psalms too, God is compared to a caring mother: 'Like a child quieted at its mother's breast; like a child that is quieted is my soul. O Israel, hope in the Lord' (Ps 131:2-3). In various passages the love of God who cares for his people is shown to be like that of a mother: thus, like a mother God 'has carried' humanity, and in particular, his Chosen People, within his own womb; he has given birth to it in travail, has nourished and comforted it (cf. Is 42:14; 46:3-4). In many passages God's love is presented as the 'masculine' love of the bridegroom and father (cf. Hos 11:1-4; Jer 3:4-19), but also sometimes as the 'feminine' love of a mother" (no. 8).

The language of "mother" is not, however, the primary

Christian language for God. Jesus called God first and foremost "Father," and so must we. We cannot be faithful to Jesus' own teaching if we depart from the manner in which he taught his disciples to pray. For the Christian, God is revealed and addressed primarily as Father, but a Father who has "motherly" qualities.

The Eye of God

Question: *I recently saw art in a church that contained the Eye of God (God's eye within a triangle). I was raised to think this was an evil symbol, not a Christian one. Please comment.*

Answer: Generally speaking, symbols have to be interpreted in context. The swastika, originally a religious symbol within Hinduism, for example, is for late-twentieth-century Jews and Christians (and most of the world, actually) a symbol of evil. The heart, on the other hand, in Christian context symbolizes divine love, charity, and compassion.

The Eye of God (an eye inside a triangle) is an ambiguous symbol. It can be good or evil depending on the purpose to which it is put. On the back of the American dollar it doesn't mean very much.

This symbol has been connected with Masonic ritual and therefore avoided by Christians. The staring eye (the "evil eye") is feared in some cultures.

Yet there exist Christian representations of the eye as symbolic of the all-knowing God. There are several biblical references to the all-seeing Eye of God: "The eyes of the LORD are toward the righteous" (Psalm 34:15); "The eyes of the LORD are in every place" (Proverbs 15:3). The use of the Eye of God in church art has an ancient (if rare) history and is quite appropriate in context.

On questions like this, we should have recourse to common sense. Symbols generally are good or evil not in themselves, but in relation to the meanings with which they are invested.

Baltimore Catechism

Question: *Where did the Baltimore Catechism come from? Is it true that it is now out of date since Vatican II? May I still read it?*

Answer: Under the official title, "Catechism of Christian Doctrine, Prepared and Enjoined by Order of the Third Council of Baltimore," the Baltimore Catechism is the product of the Plenary Council of Baltimore (Maryland) held in 1884. First published in 1885, the text was drawn up under the guidance of a committee of six bishops. The purpose of the catechism was to bring some unity to catechesis throughout the United States, a need adverted to by the American episcopate as early as 1829.

Following the publication of the original text, various other editions became available, following a variety of arrangements, so that after a few decades the Baltimore Catechism was appearing in a number of different formats.

The Baltimore Catechism is not out of date. The truths of Catholic faith do not change, and you need no one's permission to read it. Vatican II did not invalidate anything that had an authentic existence in Catholicism before the Council. What the Council did was to highlight certain truths of faith more adequately, restore the rich thought of the early Church, and bring doctrine and scripture more closely together. Those who use the Baltimore Catechism should also read the new *Catechism of the Catholic Church*. The latter is now the normative Catholic catechism. Catechists would not be wise to use the Baltimore Catechism as a primary classroom text. Vatican II did take place for a purpose (described above), and its riches and achievements require adequate expression in Catholic education and formation today.

Protestantization of Theology

Question: *Regarding the growing number of non-Catholic-trained theologians on the faculty of Catholic schools, can you explain just what is taught at such schools to distinguish Catholic from non-Catholic thinking? Theology is the study of God, is it not?*

Answer: Theology is, indeed, the study of God, but also the study of Christ, Mary, Church, grace, Eucharist, sacraments, holy orders, and ecclesiastical authority. On these matters, Catholic and Protestant theology have much in common — especially nowadays through the efforts at mutual understanding achieved through the ecumenical movement.

There do exist real differences, however, and it is natural that these show up in the different approaches to education in Catholic and Protestant theology faculties.

First, Catholic theology properly pays attention to the whole tradition of the Church over twenty centuries, while Protestant theology tends to focus on church life before the sixth and after the sixteenth centuries. A figure such as Thomas Aquinas, who is central to Catholic theology, has a much-reduced role in Protestant theology. Second, Catholic theology must have its roots firmly in divine revelation, while much present-day Protestant theology takes human experience and modern cultural concerns as the starting points. Third, unlike its Catholic counterpart, Protestant theology operates quite independently of a magisterium (teaching authority) and is not responsible to church leadership except in a limited way. Thus it tends to be more adventurous.

Doctrine of the Trinity

Question: *Can you explain the doctrine of the Trinity, and how did it find its way into the Church?*

Answer: Anyone who tries to explain the doctrine of the Trinity in a couple of paragraphs is asking for trouble. But, as they say in England, one does what one can. Trinitarian doctrine did not "find its way into the church." It was there from the beginning. We should not think that the doctrine of the Trinity was dropped from heaven one day — or invented by the Church. The Council of Nicaea, summoned in 325, gave us the Nicene Creed proclaimed at Mass every Sunday. This creed represents the most famous formulation of Trinitarian doctrine.

But before the Trinity was a doctrine it was an experience. The best place to start is with the person of Jesus. The early Christians recognized Jesus as God in human flesh in a unique and unsurpassable way. Yet in the Lord's Prayer we see Jesus teaching his disciples to pray to God the Father — as he himself did. The invisible Father, the Lord and creator of the universe, in whom the Jewish people believed, was clearly distinct from Jesus.

Then consider Pentecost. Jesus has departed from the disciples at the Ascension only to pour out his Spirit upon them in the ecstatic event of Pentecost. Though this Spirit was the Spirit of Jesus, the early Christians — and the Church in its doctrinal formulations — recognized the distinctiveness of the Spirit. The Spirit was not Jesus, though he was in Jesus.

These historical experiences were gradually formulated in the doctrine of the Trinity. In any approach to this matter, we should not think that we are dealing with dry abstractions but rather with the great wealth and richness of God's presence and activity revealed in Jesus and experienced in Christian faith.

Salvation Before Christ

Question: *The Church teaches that Jesus died for our sins so we could be saved and go to heaven. But what happened to the millions of people who lived before Christ? Where did they go?*

Answer: The matter you raise is accounted for in the article of the Apostles' Creed which says of Jesus: "He suffered under Pontius Pilate, was crucified, died, and was buried. He descended into hell. On the third day he rose again." Hell here means not the place of the damned but the abode of the dead.

The *Catechism of the Catholic Church* states: "Jesus, like all men, experienced death and in his soul joined the others in the realm of the dead" (no. 632). He descended there as Savior proclaiming the good news. "Christ went down into the depths of death so that 'the dead will hear the voice of the Son of God, and those who hear will live' " (no. 635).

The power of Christ's saving death and resurrection reaches back into the very dawn of history and forward to the end of the world, embracing all of humankind. An ancient homily for Holy Saturday has a most moving portrayal of Christ descending into the place of the dead in search of Adam and Eve, his own ancestors. You can look this up in the new *Catechism* (no. 635).

Grace and Good Works

Question: *Do you have to be in the state of grace before good works and sufferings can bear fruit for yourself or for others? Do you have to be a Roman Catholic?*

Answer: Doing good works for others in the name of Christ or offering up our sufferings in the heroic and trusting attitude of Christ are what being in the state of grace means. Grace is not a thing; it is a relationship. Good works and heroic suffering connect us to Christ and put us in his grace.

The person who is not in a state of grace loses the means to do good or to relate his or her sufferings to Christ. By the same token, doing good and living out one's difficulties with courage and faith draws one into God's grace.

Good works and redemptive suffering are possible for all men and women of goodwill, not just for Catholics or baptized Christians. The Constitution on the Church of Vatican II stated the fundamental principle on such matters: "Those who, through no fault of their own, do not know the Gospel of Christ or his Church, but who nevertheless seek God with a sincere heart, and, moved by grace, try in their actions to do his will as they know it through the dictates of their conscience — those too achieve eternal salvation" (no. 16).

Church Militant

Question: *In CCD years ago, I learned that there is the Church Militant, the Church Suffering, and the Church Triumphant. Does all that still hold?*

Answer: It certainly does, although these terms are not often used nowadays. Traditionally, the Church Militant means the church on earth struggling with temptation and battling evil, sinfulness, and imperfection. However, the term "Church Militant" (from the Latin "militia," meaning "warfare") conjures up vision of crusades, religious conflicts and inquisitions — aspects of Christian history that we would not want to repeat. Its proper meaning needs to be kept in mind.

The expression "Church Suffering" can be misleading, suggesting reference to those regions of the church under persecution (a matter, to be sure, that we should never forget). But its real reference is to Purgatory. The "Church Suffering" refers to the church of all the faithful departed who have passed into God's providence but are still being purified in Purgatory. Unfortunately, many Christians today have all but forgotten their dead brothers and sisters who are still on purgatorial pilgrimage toward Christ. Witness the poor turnout generally for Masses on All Souls' Day.

The Church Triumphant means the Church of all those who have entered into heavenly glory. This includes, in particular, the great saints. But again the word "triumphant" has a certain "in your face" ring to it that many do not (with some justification) care for today.

I would suggest the simpler terms, the Church on Earth, the Church in Purgatory, and the Church in Heaven, keeping in mind, of course, that these are not separate churches, but three *states* of the one Church of Christ.

Limbo

Question: *I am surprised to find that Limbo is not mentioned in the new* **Catechism of the Catholic Church.** *Why is this? Where does the teaching come from?*

Answer: Since the thirteenth century, Limbo (meaning "border" or "edge") has been the name used by theologians to designate the place or state reserved for infants not baptized before death, as well as the abode of the pre-Christian just awaiting the opening of Heaven by Christ. Limbo was considered a place of happiness, but lacking the vision of God.

Belief in Limbo was widely held throughout the Middle Ages and, indeed, well into the twentieth century. However, there exists no official church teaching on Limbo. The theory of Limbo was an attempt by theologians to reconcile two important principles: the desire of God that all should be saved, and the necessity of baptism for salvation.

The new *Catechism* reconciles these principles as follows (and without reference to Limbo): "As regards children who have died without Baptism, the Church can only entrust them to the mercy of God." The "great mercy of God" and "Jesus' tenderness toward children" allow us "to hope that there is a way of salvation for children who have died without Baptism" (no. 1261).

Grief Over Suicide

Question: *How can I accept the death of my 51-year-old ex-son-in-law, who committed suicide? Being a Catholic (though he was not), I pray for his soul. Every time I think of him, I cry.*

Answer: It is always difficult to accept the death of a family member or friend who has committed suicide. What can you do? First, trust in God's mercy; if you saw something good and lovable in your son-in-law, surely God sees so much more.

Second, your tears are not useless. A strand of Christian spirituality holds that when we cry, we are praying. Your tears express your love for your son-in-law.

Third, in your prayers, talk to and be reconciled with

your son-in-law. Though the earthly bond was tragically shattered, it can be renewed through the Communion of the Saints. Fourth, commit to doing some good and worthwhile work in his name. The *Catechism of the Catholic Church* states: "We should not despair of the eternal salvation of persons who have taken their own lives. By ways known to him alone, God can provide the opportunity for salutary repentance" (no. 2283).

The Rapture

Question: *Does the Catholic Church believe in the "Rapture"? Where does the idea come from?*

Answer: The term "rapture," which is generally unfamiliar to Catholics, has a popular usage among some fundamentalist Christian groups. It refers to the gathering up of the saved by Christ at the end of time. The often-quoted text here is from First Thessalonians: "The Lord himself will descend from heaven with a cry of command, with the archangel's call, and with the sound of the trumpet of God. And the dead in Christ will rise first; then we who are alive, who are left, shall be caught up together with them in the clouds to meet the Lord in the air; and so we shall always be with the Lord" (4:16-17).

This passage affirms the last judgment, the resurrection of the dead, the salvation of the living, and the reign of Christ in eternal glory. Does the Catholic Church believe in the "rapture" in this sense? Of course it does.

Some Christians who freely use the term "rapture" are inclined to think, however, that the number of those who will be saved are few and that God will destroy the earth in a great cataclysm. Preoccupation with looking for signs of the Second Coming is not unusual. From a Catholic or Orthodox

Christian point of view, these stances and concerns are unwarranted.

The Return of Christ

Question: *What is the Catholic view about when Christ will return again? Some of my Protestant friends say it will be in the year 2000? Should we worry about this?*

Answer: First, it would be strange (to say the least) if Christ's return in glory were to cause Christians to worry. The expectation that the Second Coming will be a kind of divine air raid is not well founded!

Among certain Christian groups, such as the Jehovah's Witnesses, there exists a belief in millennialism, that is, the view that Christ will return to earth for a thousand-year reign. An excessively literal reading of chapter 20 of the Book of Revelation is generally the culprit here. Such an expectation led to a lot of wild and wacky behavior as the year 1000 A.D. approached. We should not be surprised to see the same sort of thing with the advent of the third millennium.

When will Christ finally return in glory and the world come to an end? We do not know. But an important truth needs to be kept in mind: Christ is already here in hidden glory in the Church (his own body), in the Scriptures, in the sacraments, and in a privileged way in the Eucharist. This perspective should be particularly strong among Catholics. We should not envisage the end of history as the sudden and dramatic reappearance of an absent Christ, but as the action of Christ present now on earth as well as in heaven bringing creation, history, and humanity to glorious fulfillment.

Are There Cats in Heaven?

Question: *When we get to heaven, will earthly things be* *there? Are there cats in heaven? Will we know one another?*

Answer: Regarding cats in heaven, I have (as they say in the world of evasive politics) no data on that. Cats certainly do not have immortal souls.

The fundamental question here is the extent to which human relationships, achievements, and creation itself will participate in heaven.

The Second Vatican Council speaks very expressively on this matter in *Gaudium et Spes* (The Church in the Modern World). It points out that, while we do not know the way humanity or the universe will be transformed, "we are taught that God is preparing a new dwelling and a new earth in which righteousness dwells, whose happiness will fill and surpass all the desires of peace arising in the hearts of men."

In God's kingdom, "charity and its works will remain, and all of creation, which God made for man, will be set free from its bondage to decay" (no. 39).

All creation — not just souls — will be redeemed and raised up. (Read Rom 8:19-23 on this.) We can certainly expect to see those we have loved in heaven.

Why Don't Theologians Believe in Heaven?
Question: *I recently read in* Time *magazine that many theologians don't believe in heaven. Where can I find the Church's teaching on this matter? Are there any good books on heaven?*

Answer: There is no shortage of theologians who disbelieve in one or another aspect of Christian faith — a matter I wouldn't lose much sleep over.

This author will never tire of referring you to the

Catechism of the Catholic Church on matters such as this. There one will find the fundamentals of Catholic faith on heaven (see nos. 1023-1029; 1042-1050; and 325-326).

In my opinion, the best recent books on heaven are those by Peter Kreeft, titled *Heaven: The Heart's Deepest Longing* (Ignatius Press, 1989) and *Every Thing You Ever Wanted to Know About Heaven, but Never Dreamed of Asking!* (Ignatius Press, 1990).

Also, an attractive and readable account of heaven according to St. Augustine, Dante, C.S. Lewis and a host of others is found in a book titled *Journey to the Celestial City: Glimpses of Heaven from Great Literary Classics* (Moody Press, 1995), edited by Wayne Martindale.

Is the Assumption Biblical?

Question: *A non-Catholic friend of mine says that the doctrine of the Assumption has no basis in the Bible. What is the origin of the Assumption, and how should we understand it today?*

Answer: The doctrine of the Assumption is founded on three basic principles: the promise of a share in Christ's resurrection; the unique dignity of Mary as the mother of Christ; and the role of Mary as model of Christians. The biblical foundation of these principles is fairly evident to anyone who reads the New Testament with an open mind or who reflects on the general character of Christian life.

The Solemnity of the Assumption has its explicit origins in a "memorial feast" of the "falling asleep of Mary" that was widely observed throughout the Church by the sixth century. The best way to understand the Assumption is as a celebration of Mary's Easter. The Easter emphasis explains the choice of the second reading for the feast, taken from the

First Letter of Paul to the Corinthians, which declares: "For as in Adam all die, so also in Christ shall all be made alive. But each in his own order; Christ the first fruits, then at his coming those who belong to Christ" (15:22-23).

All Marian feasts and solemnities, of course, celebrate not only the person of Mary but the hope of the whole Church, of which Mary is exemplar. Accordingly, the Church looks to Mary's assumption as an anticipation of its own glorification in Christ. The preface of the Assumption Mass declares: "Today the virgin Mother of God was taken up into heaven to be the beginning and the pattern of the Church in its perfection, and a sign of hope and comfort for your people on their pilgrim way."

Mediatrix of Graces

Question: *A priest I know concludes the prayers of the faithful by saying, "We ask these and all our petitions through Mary, Mediatrix of all Graces." Doesn't this create an impression that Catholics believe that in order to obtain God's grace we must ask for it through Mary?*

Answer: The language of Mary as mediatrix has basis in Catholic tradition generally, in Vatican II, and in the teaching of Pope John Paul II. Clearly, it is consistent with Catholic faith. However, like all creatures, Mary is mediator in a manner secondary to and utterly different from that of Christ. No creature is on a par with Christ, whose mediation of salvation is unique.

To say that Mary is mediatrix or coredemptrix is to assert something authentic and essential to Catholic faith: that the salvation wrought by Christ depends on the human cooperation that has its highest expression in Mary.

However, I am among those who argue that the language

of mediatrix and coredemptrix is so misleading and so apt to be misunderstood (not only by Protestants and Orthodox, but also by Catholics themselves) that it is more trouble than it is worth. The valid points being underscored can be made in other ways.

The practice of the priest who concludes the prayers of intercession in the manner you describe is not acceptable. The Church always ends its prayers using a Trinitarian formula. Replacing such formulas is not consistent with Catholic liturgical or doctrinal tradition. Some priests add a "Hail Mary" at this point — also a practice lacking proper protocol.

Mother of God

Question: *As a convert to Catholicism, I don't understand the title of Mary as "Mother of God." I know she is the mother of Jesus, but how can God have a mother? Where does the title come from?*

Answer: As the source of all being, God, of course, does not have a mother. If he did, then she would be God (and we're not going down that avenue here!). The title you mention is shorthand for the following, more complex set of truths: Jesus is God; Mary is Jesus' physical mother; therefore Mary is acclaimed as Mother of God. St. Ignatius of Antioch (d. 107) wrote: "Our God Jesus Christ was carried in Mary's womb, according to God's plan of salvation." The title "Mother of God" became current after the third century.

This teaching was defined at the Council of Ephesus in the year 431 in response to Nestorius (d. 451) and his followers, who regarded the unity of the eternal Word of God and the humanity of Christ rather loosely and therefore viewed Mary as Mother of Christ but not of God. The Council stated that Christ was "born of the Father before the ages according to divinity, but, in the latest days, he was born of the Virgin Mary, Mother of God according to the humanity." The title "Mother of God" was therefore originally intended to safeguard the divinity of Christ.

Jesus' DNA from Mary?

Question: *Was the blood of Jesus (including, that is, his DNA) only that of Mary, or of God, too?*

Answer: Not possessing a single brain cell that understands scientific matters, I know virtually nothing about DNA. A scientist friend tells me that DNA is the genetic code unique to each person. Since Jesus was the biological son of Mary but not of Joseph, only Mary's DNA was transmitted to Jesus.

I think I am on fairly orthodox grounds (theological and scientific) when I say that God does not have DNA. The manner in which the equivalent of male DNA was contributed in the conception of Jesus is not explicable scientifically.

However, your question provides an opportunity to underline the truth of the virginal conception of Jesus by the power of the Spirit, a truth that has not only biological but theological dimensions.

The conception of Jesus through the Holy Spirit underlines the following: what the *Catechism of the Catholic Church* describes as "God's absolute initiative in the Incarnation" (no. 503); the marvelous union of the human and the divine in Jesus; the dignified vocation of motherhood; and the will of God that all men and women partake in divinity.

Papist Catholics

Question: *A number of people in our parish have been describing themselves as "Papist Catholics." What does this mean?*

Answer: The term "papist" was used in a derogatory sense in English-speaking countries by Protestants after the Reformation to designate Catholics. The term is no longer used in polite Protestant circles.

The use of this term by Catholics who wish to underline their loyalty to what they perceive to be "traditional" Catholicism is of recent vintage. The term can hardly be objected to if the purpose is to state one's deep respect for the papal office and its teaching. In that sense all real Catholics are of necessity "papists."

However, the term is sometimes used by Catholics opposed to post-Vatican II reforms or discontented with the decisions of episcopal conferences or the initiatives and decisions of the local bishop. "Papist" here can easily come to mean "more Catholic than the pope."

Catholic Feminism

Question: *Can Catholics believe in "feminism"? I read that the Pope has said positive things about feminism. Is that true?*

Answer: I understand feminism to be a movement to advance the roles of women in church and society in ways that are positive and productive. Accordingly, Catholics not only may but should believe in (and practice) feminism.

I would, however, admit that there are many other ways to define feminism, as well as many kinds of feminism, not all of them compatible with Catholicism. It is difficult, for instance, to see how a feminism founded on Marxism could be consistent with Catholicism. For some Catholic commentators, the term "feminism" has an entirely negative connotation and is incapable of being "baptized" Christian, so to speak.

Pope John Paul has indeed spoken positively about

feminism. In his 1995 encyclical "The Gospel of Life" (*Evangelium Vitae*), Pope John Paul II spoke of a "new feminism" which would "affirm the true genius of women in every aspect of the life of society" (no. 99). The pope's more extensive thinking in this area is found in his apostolic letter "On the Dignity and Vocation of Women" (*Mulieris Dignitatem*).

A genuine Catholic feminism places a high priority on women's dignity, the equality of women and men, the value of marriage and the family, the cultural contribution of women, and it would be strongly pro-life. Authentic Catholic feminism rejects the individualistic and competitive characteristics of some strands of North American feminism.

Liberation Theology

Question: *I am confused about liberation theology. Our pastor is all for it, but our assistant pastor says the Church disapproves of it. Please comment.*

Answer: Liberation theology emerged in Latin America in the late 1960s as a means of bringing the Gospel and the Church more systematically and consciously into the struggle for human rights, economic development, and social justice. There exists, however, no single school of liberation theology, but rather a variety of perspectives and outlooks.

In its official teaching, the Church has had both positive and critical things to say about liberation theology. These are found in two Instructions from the Vatican Congregation for the Doctrine of the Faith: one in 1984 named, "On Certain Aspects of the Theology of Liberation," and one in 1986 entitled, "On Christian Freedom and Liberation."

Liberation theologies that use the Gospel and Catholic social teaching as their starting point are generally on secure ground and are more apt to be favored by the Church. Theologies of liberation based on secular theories of history and economics (such as those provided by Marxism) are what the Church has in mind when it criticizes liberation theology.

Liberation theology has, in the view of many (including myself), made a positive contribution to Catholic social teaching. But like all new theological trends, it is capable of errors and excesses.

What Is Relativism?

Question: *I read that the Pope recently wrote a document against relativism. Please explain what relativism means.*

Answer: Relativism is an outlook which holds that all truth, including religious truth, lacks certainty because so much about human knowledge is questionable.

In an age in which scientific data, arguments, and conclusions are highly prized, it is not surprising that some people nowadays (mostly in academic and media circles) are skeptical about intangibles like God, salvation, and eternal life (about which, after all, there exist no scientific certainties).

Religious and philosophical truths are the most obvious objects of relativism. Since religions make conflicting truth claims — and (if they are worth their salt) often highly competing ones — it is easy to dismiss religious claims.

Many people think they believe that all religions are equal (actually nobody really believes this) and that moral standards are based on individual conscience alone (a principle most people don't actually practice: our society is not relativistic about child abuse, burglary, or kidnapping, for instance). Yet one only has to watch a couple of TV talk shows to see how pervasive in our society is the relativistic outlook, even if it does not always square with the actual practical lives of most people.

Relativism was a theme in *Fides et Ratio*, an encyclical published by Pope John Paul II in 1998. In that document the Pope defended the notion of the objectivity of truth and the possibility that truth is accessible to the human intellect. The Pope fears that relativism leads to irrationalism and to the breakdown of intellectual traditions — in other words, to chaos.

Pelagianism

Question: *In his homilies, our pastor says that American Catholics are modern-day Pelagians. Please explain the origin of this term.*

Answer: Pelagianism refers to the heretical teaching on grace of Pelagius (355-425), a native of England who "made a name for himself" in Rome. Pelagius objected to St. Augustine's strong emphasis on the need for grace if one is to be saved. Pelagius thought Augustine played down the human person's use of free will.

Pelagius, who wrote and spoke extensively, was condemned by Church councils during his lifetime, notably the Councils of Carthage and Mileve in 416. The decisions of these councils were confirmed the following year by Pope Innocent I. Pelagius deceived the next Pope, Zosimus, who at first exonerated him but in 418 retracted his decision.

Pelagianism is a mixture of doctrinal views which have reappeared in Christianity over the centuries. Among its principal expressions are the belief that Adam would have died whether he had sinned or not; that Adam's sin injured himself alone and only affected his descendants by giving bad example; that newborn children are in the same condition of grace as Adam before he sinned; that humankind does not die because of Adam's sin or rise because of Christ's resurrection; that the law of ancient Israel no less than the Gospel offers equal opportunity to reach heaven; and that before the coming of Christ there existed people without sin.

A generalization that American Catholics are Pelagians is, in my view, not fully warranted. However, whenever there occurs an inadequate emphasis on human sin, the playing down of God's judgment, a belief in humanity's self-perfectibility, or the conviction that human beings can pull themselves into God's kingdom by their own bootstraps, then Pelagian tendencies are present. This general perspective is more likely to be found today among liberal Protestants than Catholics.

Modernism

Question: *I hear a lot of talk these days in the Church about modernism. People call others "modernists." Please explain what this means? What is wrong with the Church being modern?*

Answer: The current trend of people calling others "modernists" is mostly mud-slinging. The term is popularly synonymous with "progressive" or "liberal." The opposing side is called "conservative," "traditionalist" or (more recently) "fundamentalist." Most of these terms are fairly useless because they are so ill-defined (not to say often motivated by a lack of charity).

Technically speaking, modernism refers to a theory about the nature of Christian faith associated with figures including George Tyrrell (died 1909) and Alfred Loisy (died 1940). These thinkers were part of a movement to reconcile Christian faith with modern philosophical and scientific thought.

Modernism was thought by its critics to hold a highly subjective view of religion in which experience of the divine comes from within the human person and defies adequate doctrinal expression. Objective revelation is virtually denied in such a perspective.

Modernism was condemned by Pope Pius X in two documents, *Lamentabili* and *Pascendi*, both published in 1907.

Whether modernism really existed or not has been a matter of debate in recent decades. In any case, the kind of views rejected by Pius X are not compatible with authentic Catholic faith. The Church continues to be vigilant about their reappearance today.

There is nothing wrong with the Church being modern, if by this is meant that the Church should understand modern thought and culture and seek to minister effectively in relation to these. However, where modern ideas and thought patterns inconsistent with Christian tradition begin to undermine the latter, then modernism as an "ism" is at work.

Gnosticism

Question: *I read a lot about gnosticism but don't really understand what it means. Are there gnostics today? What about Christian gnostics?*

Answer: Gnosticism is a heresy (ancient, yet ever new) which holds that the way to salvation is by acquiring knowledge. This knowledge is received not from an external, authoritative source, but from private interior revelation accessible only to a few. Given this outlook, gnosticism is generally elitist.

From ancient times, there existed gnostics who claimed to know the mysteries of the universe. Gnosticism made some inroads into early Christian circles but was vehemently opposed by orthodox Christianity. Christian gnostics borrowed freely from the four Gospels, but also wrote new ones of their own. In general, gnosticism proposed a dualistic system of belief, meaning that matter was thought to be hostile to spirit.

Although extinct as an organized religion, gnosticism shows up today in the New Age and other such movements. Because it denies objective biblical revelation and holds that Christ did not establish a church or a teaching authority, gnostically-minded people tend to float away from Christianity toward more privatized and self-obsessed forms of religion. Present-day American forms of gnosticism are fairly dippy.

Materialism

Question: *If God created the world, why is "materialism" such a bad thing? Aren't materialists taking creation more seriously than some religious people?*

Answer: Materialism is the theory that all reality is reducible to matter and has its foundation in matter. No proper distinction between matter and spirit is allowed in the materialistic outlook. Even the human soul is thought to be material.

Materialism holds that created things, human activity, and emotional experiences, serve a purely non-transcendental end. In social thought, materialism refers to the view that economic and political interests are the principal concerns of society.

Contrary to what one might expect, materialists do not take the created order more seriously than those with a well-balanced religious outlook. They take it less seriously. The biblical view that God created the world and everything therein means that people of faith view matter as holy, to be revered as a sign of God's goodness and beauty. Materialists espouse a merely pragmatic view of creation.

Creation-Centered Spirituality

Question: *There is a lot of talk in our parish adult education* *programs about creation-centered spirituality. Is such a spirituality really Catholic?*

Answer: There exist a variety of creation spiritualities, some more consistent with Catholic tradition than others. What the different spiritualities of creation have in common is a reverence for the earth as God's handwork, a view of creation as revelatory of the glory of God, opposition to the misuse and exploitation of nature, and an appreciation of work and art as modes of participation in God's creative activity.

This general perspective is admirable and deserves to be promoted. It has strong roots in the Scriptures, and in figures like St. Benedict, St. Francis of Assisi, St. Hildegarde of Bingen, and Julian of Norwich. It is also well developed in Eastern Christian theology.

There is, however, a type of creation theology (associated with Matthew Fox, Thomas Berry, and Rosemary Ruether) that is quite difficult to reconcile with Catholic tradition in that it accords an inadequate role to the reality of sin, redemption, revelation, and the person of Christ. Authentic Christian spirituality must of necessity be centered not on creation, but on the Trinity, Christ, the Church, and the sacraments. Where there exists a proper focus on these, a positive theology of creation can, indeed, be richly incorporated into Christian thought and practice.

Modern Pagans

Question: *I saw a sign at one of our neighborhood churches that announced "pagan services." Are pagans an organized religion in America? What does "pagan" mean?*

Answer: The term "pagan" comes from the Latin "paganus," meaning countryman, villager, or civilian. The word was originally used to describe anyone who did not profess belief in the oneness of God. For Christians, Jews, and Muslims the term meant a person who does not believe in the God of biblical revelation. More generally, a pagan is a person who has abandoned religious belief and practice.

Today the term "pagan" is rarely used (although when my sister was preparing for her wedding in the Irish midlands in the late 1980s, her parish priest referred in my presence to her unbaptized New Zealander fiancé as "a lovely lad, for a pagan").

There is some resurgence of organized paganism in North America these days — but I have the impression that it's not an overly organized movement. Present-day pagan communities generally focus their credal allegiances on wild parties, singing in the woods at 3:00 A.M., and a fairly relaxed sexual morality.

Jehovah's Witnesses

Question: *Are the Jehovah's Witnesses a "Christian" group? Why did you use this definition to describe the sect? They deny the Holy Trinity and the divinity of Jesus Christ.*

Answer: The term "Christian" may be used in at least two ways. At its broadest, it means any group that claims to follow Christ or for whom Christ is a central figure.

The term may also be used in a second and more strict sense to describe a group or community that follows orthodox belief in Christ as expressed by the early councils and traditional Christian creeds.

Nothing is compromised by recognizing that in the broader sense Jehovah's Witnesses are Christian. The theology of the group does purport to be Christian and is focused on the New Testament. Holding heretical theological views about Christ does not invalidate a claim to be Christian in a general moral or spiritual sense.

Catholicism does, however, have difficulty in describing Jehovah's Witnesses as Christian in the second stricter sense. The theology of God and of Christ held by Witnesses is notably inconsistent with that of mainstream Christianity.

To pick another example from my own state of Utah: It, is, in my opinion, rash to deny that Mormonism is Christian in a broad moral and spiritual sense. Yet Mormons would not claim to be Christian in the theological manner understood by Catholic, Protestant, and Orthodox Christians and are not in continuity (nor do they wish to be) with historic Christianity.

Horoscopes

Question: *Could you please touch on the topic of horoscopes, which are popular in Spain, with people paying all sorts of attention to them in the newspapers each day of the year and trying to believe and live according to the predictions given?*

Answer: I must admit that occasionally I read my horoscope in the newspaper (usually on slow news days), but like most people — you'll be glad to hear — I do not take them too seriously. Horoscope predictions like, "Today, something unexpected will happen to you" are hardly revealing or life-altering.

However, when people do take horoscopes seriously, there is a problem. The *Catechism of the Catholic Church* rejects (as one would expect), magic, sorcery, occultism, and divination — by which is meant recourse to Satan or demons, conjuring up the dead, and attempting to "unveil" the future (see nos. 2115-2117). The *Catechism* states: "Consulting horoscopes, astrology, palm reading, interpretation of omens and lots, the phenomena of clairvoyance, and recourse to mediums all conceal a desire for power over time, history, and, in the last analysis, other human beings, as well as a wish to conciliate hidden powers. They contradict the honor, respect, and loving fear that we owe to God alone" (no. 2116). Most people I know who read horoscopes invest no weight in them, but merely read them for fun. However, heavy-duty horoscope reading is unbecoming of Christians.

Prophecies of St. Malachy

Question: *I recently came across information about the Prophecies of St. Malachy which tell us that there are only two popes left after Pope John Paul II. Do you think these prophecies will come true?*

Answer: If the so-called "Prophecies of St. Malachy" come true, it won't be because of any divine inspiration guiding them. These "Prophecies," which list 102 popes and 10 antipopes (claimants to the papacy), are found in a spurious document falsely attributed to St. Malachy, archbishop of the ancient see of Armagh in Ireland, who died in 1148. Generally regarded as a forgery by an unknown author, the document appears to be from the latter part of the 16th century.

The first block of prophecies covers the 65 popes and 10 antipopes from Celestine II (1143-1144) to Gregory XIV (1590-91). The material is fairly exact with regard to the names, birthplaces, titles, and other particular characteristics of the personages described. Far from being prophetic, in the sense of seeing into the future, this section of the work is the result of historical data in the possession of the astute author. The 37 descriptions of popes following the reign of

Gregory XIV are rather vague and esoteric, and they lend themselves to meaning whatever the reader wants them to mean. According to the prophecies, the present pope will have only two successors before the end of the world.

There is no shortage of religious literature of this sort. It's the kind of stuff you might read for entertainment on a boring airline flight, but it deserves the same level of credibility as your horoscope (that is to say, none).

Dreams

Question: *I often have strange dreams, sometimes on religious themes. How seriously should I take them?*

Answer: If I took every strange dream I ever had (including those on religious themes) seriously, I would be out of my mind by now. The night before writing this answer, I dreamt that someone drove a car at high speed up the main aisle of our cathedral and crashed it deliberately into the back wall of the sanctuary. (A "conservative" friend said I should interpret this as a divine warning about the dire consequence of the absence of altar rails in churches.)

Two points may be made about dreams. First, dreams are a legitimate source of revelation (though I don't think mine was!). Both the Old and New Testaments tell of divinely-inspired dreams. We need only think of the dreams which led St. Joseph to take the Christ child to Egypt and the Wise Men to return from Bethlehem by another route. However, only the community of the Church can formally recognize dreams as of significant value — and in retrospect.

Most dreams are so confused, disorganized, and topsy-turvy, and so affected by what's going on in our lives, that they should be given no more credence than one's horoscope.

If a dream helps you gain positive insight into your life or makes you a better Christian, good. If it disrupts your life and drives people around you crazy, then you may want to ask your doctor about a friend who has strange religious dreams.

Levitation

Question: *What do you think of levitation? Does the Church approve of it?*

Answer: Never having seen levitation (or experienced it myself), my thinking on the matter is quite undeveloped. Levitation refers to the phenomenon in which a human body — without any natural support — is raised completely above the ground and suspended in thin air.

Stories of levitation are reported in the lives of some saints, including Francis Xavier, Paul of the Cross, and Philip Neri. Among the most celebrated cases is St. Joseph of Cupertino, a seventeenth-century Franciscan, who was treated sternly by his superiors because of the disturbances his reported levitations caused. Joseph was popularly know as the "flying friar."

According to Pope Benedict XIV (1740-58), the verification of a genuine levitation requires a thorough investigation to eliminate a natural explanation or fraud.

Levitation is not a central factor in Christian life. It belongs in the category of the paranormal (that is, outside normal life). The Church places little emphasis on the phenomenon, is very cautious in its approach to claims about it, but is open-minded enough not to exclude the possibility of extraordinary occurrences of this type.

Being the subject of levitation does not necessarily demonstrate personal sanctity or virtue; it demonstrates only the ability to be levitated. There could, in fact, be something demonic to a particular incidence.

Symbolically, levitation has some connection to events

like the Ascension and the Assumption (complex phenomena in themselves) and it dramatizes the heavenly destiny of God's children.

Telepathy

Question: *Do you believe in telepathy? My wife does and she is driving me crazy! She says she is telepathic. She says her mother is, too.*

Answer: I have never given telepathy much thought. I believe in the possibility of anything that is not self-contradictory. The phenomenon you mention refers to the transmission of information from one mind to another without any of the ordinary means of communication.

While science is generally skeptical of such possibilities, serious commentators have suggested that telepathic means of communicating knowledge involving extraordinary personalities have been known to occur.

Instances of the communication of thought without verbal or physical means are recorded in the lives of some saints. However, the Church does not hold that such occurrences, even when verified, are always a reliable sign of virtue.

Whether your wife is driving you nuts generally or because she claims telepathic powers, you do not say. The best approach is to judge her claims by their results. If the results are destructive, disruptive, or troublesome, then you are right to be bothered by them. By the same token, if your mother-in-law is able to account for your every move, you really do have serious trouble on your plate. However, if the claims to telepathy are harmless or benign, then I would be thankful for small mercies.

TWO

Scripture

General
Old Testament
New Testament

Sources of Faith

Question: *Other than faith and the Bible, what reasons do we have and why do we believe in God?*

Answer: The *Catechism of the Catholic Church* is excellent on this matter. I recommend nos. 26-35, which deal with the natural disposition of the human person to know and seek God. If the human person is made in the image of God he or she is by nature a religious seeker. Because we are children of God, we are able to see the divine in each other. Since God is the author and sustainer of creation, then God is capable of being glimpsed in creation itself.

God's self-revelation in his Son, Jesus Christ — known to us through the Church, the sacraments and the Bible — is, of course, the central and most important means by which we know God, but these media of divine revelation have their wider setting in creation itself. God is not alien to his creation. In a certain sense, we might say that creation and history have a sacramental quality. They reveal to us something of God. Humankind has the capacity to deduce the existence of God from the order, beauty, and coherence of created things.

Proselytizing Brother

Question: *Since I became a Catholic, my Protestant brother is convinced that I'm going to hell. I love him very much and enjoy his company when we discuss topics other than religion. Every time I visit, he produces his Bible and points to Scriptures which he claims the Catholic Church violates. His concern for my soul is rooted in sibling love. How can I deal with this and keep our friendship?*

Answer: It sounds to me that your brother is not the kind of person you can easily reason with. You are, of course, perfectly right to want to maintain your good relationship with him.

I propose that you handle the matter as follows: (1) Tell your brother of your love and affection for him and your desire not to let matters of religion come between you. (2) Express to him your respect for the sincerity of his faith and your appreciation for the concern he has for your salvation. (3) Tell him that his best hope for your salvation is not through contentious argument, but through his fervent prayer for you. (This last suggestion is a little clever — as he will expect God to lead you back to your faith of origin, while you know God won't.) A mixture of firmness, kindness, and astuteness is the only way to go.

Douai Bible

Question: *What is the Douai Bible? How does it differ from new Bibles? Is the Douai version out of date?*

Answer: The Douai (sometimes spelt Douay) Bible is an English translation of the Scriptures prepared at the English College, Douai, Belgium, founded in 1568. The English College was later moved to Rheims, where the New Testament was completed and published in 1582, resulting in the Douai-Rheims version. The Old Testament was published in 1609 after the English College had returned to Douai.

The translation, driven more by concern for accuracy than for poetic style, was made from the Latin Vulgate, but carefully following the original Hebrew and Greek. The work was mainly the undertaking of Gregory Martin (who died in 1582). In the eighteenth century, this Bible was considerably revised by English Bishop Challoner. Until the middle of the twentieth century, this version was commonly used by English-speaking Catholics worldwide.

Newer versions of the Bible do not invalidate works like

the Douai Bible. However, more recent Bibles have a number of advantages. They provide more technically exact translations (a matter of little practical consequence for the average reader); their twentieth-century language is obviously more accessible; and they benefit from common ecumenical scholarship in the area of scripture studies.

What Are the Four "Senses" of Scripture?

Question: *In a homily, our pastor recently mentioned the "four senses" of Scripture. Can you explain this?*

Answer: There have been in history many rich and profound ways of interpreting Scripture, among them advertence to the "four senses" you mentioned.

The language is complicated (the literal sense, the allegorical sense, the moral sense, and the anagogical sense), but the meaning is not. Let us take the Book of Isaiah for instance. The book may be read on four levels.

First, it represents the historic dreams and hopes of Isaiah in his own time and circumstances (the literal sense). Second, it may be interpreted as fulfilled in Christ (read Luke 4:16-22). Third, it is appropriately understood as indicating the ongoing vocation of the Church and of Christians today (the moral sense). Fourth, it may be regarded as referring to God's work of redemption to be fulfilled at the end of time (the anagogical sense).

Another way is to say that Scripture passages may be read historically, Christologically, ecclesiologically, and eschatologically. Consult the *Catechism of the Catholic Church* on this matter (nos. 115-119).

Biblical Criticism

Question: *I read a lot about biblical criticism even in Catholic papers. Why would good Catholics want to criticize the Bible?*

Answer: The word "criticism" has both popular and technical meanings. Popularly, criticism means negative commentary. Technically, it means to make careful judgment about something or to study a matter scientifically.

People can be critical of the Bible in the popular sense (as in, "I think the Bible is nonsense") or in the technical sense. In the latter sense, biblical criticism means the study and analysis of the Bible in its historical, literary, and theological aspects.

Critical study of this kind has been encouraged and fostered by ecclesiastical leadership, especially in the twentieth century. Two important papal documents in modern times urging Catholic scholars to engage in careful scientific study of the Bible were *Providentissimus Deus*, issued by Pope Leo XIII in 1893, and *Divino Afflante Spiritu*, published by Pope Pius XII in 1943.

Biblical criticism in the Catholic Church starts from the recognition that the Bible is the inspired word of God and not merely the product of human imagination. However, the inspired word is written in human words. Thus the Church is concerned that the Scriptures be carefully and accurately understood, translated, and transmitted.

Religion and Myth

Question: *During an Advent series in our parish, the speaker kept referring to the "Christian myth." He seemed to mean the Bible. How can one call the Scriptures myth and still be Catholic?*

Answer: I can't vouch for the speaker, but (to put the best face on the matter), one can distinguish between two very different meanings of the word "myth." The first meaning is a story that is ill-founded, has little or no basis in history, or is simply untrue. That St. Patrick drove snakes from Ireland and that Santa Claus visits every child at Christmas are myths in this particular sense. (I hope no child is reading this.)

The second meaning of myth is a highly embellished or ornamented story with a basis in history that reveals to us a divine truth. The stories of creation in the Bible may, in this sense, be spoken of as myth. The creation stories are not newspaper accounts, but divinely-inspired stories that are meant to reveal to us God's authorship of creation.

People who speak of Bible stories as myth in the first sense are dismissing them as fairy tales. But to speak of biblical accounts as mythological in the second sense is to say that the stories reveal divine truth using highly symbolic language.

Only the second sense of the word "myth" may ever be correctly used when speaking of Bible stories.

Religious Numbers

Question: *A Baptist neighbor told me that the Catholic Church has a lot of secret numbers. How should I answer her?*

Answer: Try a little humor. Ask her if she knows why Catholic bishops wear little purple skullcaps? (Answer: to hide the 666 mark imprinted on their skulls.) If you are not the jovial type and/or she has no sense of the ridiculous, you could respond politely: "That is very interesting; thank you for telling me" and quickly change the subject to something more profound — like the special lunch deal this week at your local Donut Warehouse.

There is nothing necessarily esoteric about symbolic numbers. They are found in the Bible itself. They have naturally become part of Christian liturgy and art.

For instance, three is the number of persons in the Trinity and of the days Christ spent in the tomb. Seven is the symbolic number of the gifts the Holy Spirit, the seven sacraments, the seven deadly sins, and the seven sorrows of Mary.

Sunday is called the eighth day, the day beyond all days, the day of eternity. For this reason baptism fonts often have an octagonal shape.

Fifty symbolizes the fulfillment of divine promise. In Judaic history the feast of Pentecost was celebrated fifty days after the Passover and commemorated the giving of the Law to Moses. The Holy Spirit promised by Christ descended upon the apostles on the fiftieth day after Easter.

One hundred means plenitude, and one thousand means a number too immense to be counted.

There are numerous other symbolic numbers in the Bible and Christian liturgy having perfectly edifying and reasonable meanings. Thoughtful and well-educated minds tend not to search out dark and sinister significances.

Apocrypha

Question: *I know that the "Apocrypha" refers to six books of the Old Testament officially accepted as Divine Scripture by the Catholic Church but rejected by Protestantism. Did the Catholic Church only officially sanction these books after the Protestant Reformation at the Council of Trent, or were they considered Divine Scripture all along?*

Answer: This matter can be confusing because Catholics and Protestants mean different things by "Apocrypha." In the interests of avoiding confusion, I will use "Apocrypha" here in the way Protestants do (which is what you seem to have in mind). As we all know (don't we?), the Protestant Bible has 66 books, while the Catholic has 73 books. The difference in number involves the set of writings Protestants call "Apocrypha." These books had always been in use in the

Catholic Church, although there were some early disputes about them. This longstanding usage became formalized in the sixteenth century at the Council of Trent in response to the Protestant Reformers, who disputed the authenticity of the books in question.

The rejection of the so-called "Apocrypha" by the Reformers was founded partly on Protestant opposition to certain Catholic dogmas and practices (including the doctrine of purgatory and Masses for the dead). In fixing the Canon of Scripture to include what Protestants reject as "Apocrypha," the Council of Trent was not at all being innovative, but was simply recognizing in a formal way the tradition of the Church from the very beginning. Since some Protestant Bibles nowadays print the "Apocrypha," the matter is not as contentious as it once was.

Earth Day

Question: *An observance of Earth Day held recently at a local university included music, art, prayer, and Scripture focused on environmental and ecological issues related to the four elements of fire, air, water, and earth. It all sounded rather pagan to me. Please comment.*

Answer: Concern for material creation is perfectly consistent with biblical faith. God himself is the creator of heaven and earth. We read in Genesis that "God saw everything that he had made, and behold, it was very good" (1:31). Genesis also states that at the very beginning God gave humankind stewardship of creation (see 1:28-30). The Psalms call on all creation to praise God. Look up, for instance, Psalm 148. Think of a hymn like "All Creatures of Our God and King," which rouses the created world to give glory to God.

The four elements of creation you mention feature

prominently in Catholic liturgy and spirituality. In the sacrament of baptism, water is made holy. The Easter Vigil begins with a blessing of fire. Earth is dedicated before a dead body is laid in it. Air symbolizes the invisible motions of the Holy Spirit.

"Liturgies" are pagan if creation is interpreted and regarded in a pagan way (that is to say, one inconsistent with Christianity). They are obviously Christian if the elements of the earth are understood in a Christian manner such as I have just suggested.

Sunday or Sabbath?

Question: *I always heard that Sunday was the Sabbath Day. A Seventh-Day Adventist told me this is not true. Please comment.*

Answer: Sunday has never been properly regarded by Christians as the Sabbath day. The Old Testament Sabbath occurred on the seventh day of the week, not the first. We read in Exodus: "The seventh day is a sabbath of solemn rest, holy to the LORD" (31:15). In the first six days, God created the world, "and on the seventh day he rested" (31:17). Right up to the present, the Jewish people observe Saturday as the Sabbath.

According to all the Gospels, Jesus rose from the dead on the "first" day of the week, that is, the day after the Sabbath. The early Christians often spoke of Sunday as the "eighth day," that is the day beyond all days, the day which symbolizes eternity.

The *Catechism of the Catholic Church* states that Sunday is the "fulfillment" of the Sabbath. We read: "Sunday is expressly distinguished from the Sabbath which it follows chronologically every week; for Christians its ceremonial observance replaces that of the Sabbath. In Christ's Passover,

Sunday fulfills the spiritual truth of the Jewish Sabbath and announces man's eternal rest in God" (no. 2175).

Your Seventh-Day Adventist friend is correct. But he or she isn't exactly scoring a point. While in Catholicism, Sunday has been (and still is) often loosely referred to as the Sabbath, there has always existed the recognition that Sunday differs from the Old Testament Sabbath and that the obligation to keep holy the Sabbath day was, by Christ's resurrection, transferred to Sunday.

Manna

Question: *I read recently that the Manna from heaven that the Israelites received from God was not miraculous—but only bread-like stuff that grows naturally in the desert. Is this true?*

Answer: "Manna" is the name given in the Bible for the miraculous food which fed the Israelites in the desert during their journey to the promised land (see Exodus 16:1-36; Numbers 11:4-9).

There are three ways to approach the matter you describe. One is to insist that the manna was a supernatural material literally dropped from heaven. The second is to hold (along the lines you mention) that the event has a completely natural, non-miraculous explanation. It is well known that the tamarisk tree in the Egyptian desert exudes a bread-like substance that is edible. The third approach is to hold that God's providence often works through natural phenomena and circumstances.

Could the manna have been a natural substance? Yes; the biblical texts do not tell us of its composition. Does this mean it did not have a miraculous character? No, it does not.

There are truly supernatural miracles (the virgin birth,

the resurrection of Jesus), but there are also natural miracles: God acting providentially through nature ("miracle drugs"; the strength to survive a tragedy).

Given the lack of specific data in Exodus and Numbers about the "manna," one is free to adopt either the natural or supernatural explanation. However, the fundamental point or moral of the story is not optional: that the Israelites really and truly did encounter God's providence and were decisively saved from starvation.

Ark of the Covenant

Question: *What happened to the Ark of the Covenant mentioned in the Bible? Does it still exist somewhere?*

Answer: The Ark of the Covenant was the sacred chest containing the tablets of the Ten Commandments given to Moses. God instructed Moses to construct the ark of acacia wood and provided him with exact dimensions: 4 feet long, 2-1/2 feet wide and 2-1/2 feet high (see Ex 25:10-22; 37:1-9).

The Ark of the Covenant became a most venerated object in Israelite history. It accompanied the people on their wilderness journeys and into the Promised Land. Later it was seized by the Philistines, who surrendered it back to Israel out of superstition. (Besides, the Philistines didn't have much appreciation for nice stuff, anyway.) David brought the Ark to Jerusalem, where it remained until the temple was destroyed in 587 B.C. At that point it disappeared from history.

In the Christian order of things, the Church itself is regarded as the new dwelling place of God, the new Ark. In the Litany of Loreto, Mary is called "Ark of the Covenant," since she was the bearer of Christ. The Ark may be said to be wherever God dwells: in his people, in the Word, in the sacraments — especially the Eucharist.

Tabernacles in churches are sometimes designed in a style based on the dimensions and character of the original Ark of the Covenant.

Guardian Angels

Question: *Where did the teaching on guardian angels come from? Is this teaching found in the Bible?*

Answer: Guardian angels are heavenly beings sent by God to accompany and watch over each person during his or her earthly life. The belief in guardian angels is part of the long tradition of the Church. It is based in the Scriptures and the teaching of the early Christian Fathers.

The existence of angels generally is mentioned in numerous places in the Old and New Testaments. Look up the *Catechism of the Catholic Church* for references (nos. 328-334). Regarding guardian angels in particular, Catholic tradition holds that "From infancy to death, human life is surrounded by their watchful care and intercession" (*Catechism*, no. 336). St. Basil wrote, "Beside each believer stands an angel as protector and shepherd leading him to life" (see *Catechism, ibid.*).

The role of the guardian angel is to guide the person to good thoughts, words, and works, and to preserve him or her from evil. Since the seventeenth century, a feast honoring the guardian angels has been celebrated throughout the universal Church. In the revised calendar the feast is observed on October 2.

Archangel Raphael

Question: *I know about the archangels Gabriel and Michael but I know very little about Raphael. Can you fill me in? Why is Raphael so little known?*

Answer: Because Raphael did not have, shall we say, the same high career profile as Gabriel (who announced to Mary she would be the mother of God), and Michael (who cast Lucifer and the fallen angels from heaven). Raphael is more of a generalist among the archangels.

The Archangel Raphael has traditionally been regarded as the protector of the young, pilgrims, and travelers. Raphael is also linked with healing because his name in Hebrew means "God heals."

Raphael appears in the Bible in the Book of Tobit. Therein, he is the guardian of journeys (see Tb 5-6); a healer (Tb 6; 11:1-15); and the one who expels demons (Tb 6:15-17; 8:1-3). He is among the seven special angels who offer the prayers of God's people and enter into the presence of the Holy One (Tb 12:15).

Raphael became a popular figure in the apocryphal Book of Enoch, in which he plays a number of roles. He heals the illnesses and injuries of humankind. Interestingly, he is also charged with the healing of the earth, which has been injured by human sin and the fallen angels. Raphael is told: "And give life to the earth which the angels have corrupted. And he will proclaim to the earth, that he is giving life to her" (Enoch 10:7).

Old Testament Saints?

Question: *New Testament believers are called "saints." The Letter to the Hebrews lists Old Testament figures as part of the great "cloud of witnesses." But we never address Old Testament figures as saints. Why is this?*

Answer: Your question raises the larger issue of the way the term "saint" is used. Three usages may be identified.

First, there is the category of saints who are canonized,

that is, formally recognized by the Church for outstanding holiness. The term was used in this specific sense from the fifth century onwards. Mary, the apostles, and the martyrs comprised the original membership of this category.

Second, the word "saint" has a more popular reference to holy men and women generally. Though not canonized, many Christians are notable examples of virtue. We often hear people describe a family member, friend, or neighbor as a "saint." Some use the term "saint" of people like Mother Teresa of Calcutta.

The third meaning of "saint" is the original one. In the New Testament, Paul uses the word for every baptized person (see Rom 1:7; 1 Cor 1:2). All Christians are called into the communion of saints in baptism. Today Mormons use the term "saint" in this very general sense (which is not a good reason for Catholics to reject such practice!).

The great Old Testament figures are not saints in the first sense. Since they lived before Christ, they could not realistically be regarded as outstanding examples of Christian holiness. However, they might be considered saints in the second (more popular) sense. Old Testament figures are traditionally venerated in Christian art. Orthodox churches are sometimes named after personages from the Old Testament (Elijah, for instance).

St. Joseph

Question: *In the Bible the last thing written about St. Joseph was that he and Mary found Jesus in the temple. You would think that scholars would have kept track of this man. What do we know about St. Joseph?*

Answer: Indeed, very little is known about St. Joseph. Yet from a spiritual perspective we know plenty: that he was the loving husband of Mary, the foster father of Jesus, and that he did his best to care for and protect Mary and her Son.

Pope John Paul II issued in 1989 an apostolic exhortation on St. Joseph entitled "Guardian of the Redeemer" (*Redemptoris Custos*). Your local Catholic bookstore can order a copy for you.

In this extended meditation, the pope reflects thoughtfully on St. Joseph as a husband, a model of work, and a contemplative. Pope John Paul reiterates Pius IX's declaration of St. Joseph as "patron of the Catholic Church," a title that reflects Joseph's fatherly care for Jesus and Mary.

The Jesus Seminar

Question: *I have heard a lot recently about a group called "the Jesus Seminar" and the fact that some theologians think most of the Gospels may not be reliable. Where can I find out more about this?*

Answer: The Jesus Seminar is a small association of biblical scholars from various denominations who have been meeting about twice yearly since 1985 to determine what may reliably be known about the historical Jesus. Their answer is: not much. The Seminar members have concluded that the number of actual sayings of Jesus that should be regarded as authentic are very few indeed. The Seminar scholars vote about these matters in highly publicized arenas using a somewhat showy procedure.

The vast majority of Scripture scholars — even very "liberal" ones — do not think much of the Jesus Seminar. If you want to know more about the work of this group, you could read the book called *The Real Jesus* by Luke Timothy Johnson — which offers a highly critical evaluation of the

Jesus Seminar. The book's subtitle is "The Misguided Quest for the Historical Jesus and the Truth of the Traditional Gospels." Johnson's book is incisive, smartly written, and very entertaining.

Ever Virgin

Question: *I always believed that the words "ever virgin" meant that Mary was a virgin throughout her life. But on "Mysteries of the Bible" on TV, some theologians claimed that after Jesus' birth Mary had relations with Joseph and had other children. Is this correct?*

Answer: You should take TV programs like "Mysteries of the Bible" with a pinch of salt. Catholic teaching holds that Mary is to be venerated as "ever-Virgin." She was such before and after the birth of Jesus.

There has been no lack of commentators in Christian history who have questioned this belief.

The theological opinion you mention often points for support to Gospel references to "brothers" and "sisters" of Jesus. The Church has always understood these to mean Jesus' cousins or close relatives. In Matthew's Gospel, James and Joseph are referred to as "brothers of Jesus" (13:55). But these, in fact, are the sons of someone Matthew later calls "the other Mary" (28:1; cf. 27:56).

Read the *Catechism of the Catholic Church* on this matter (nos. 496-507). And always keep a good-sized carton of salt on your TV tray.

Son of Man

Question: *Our RCIA instructor says that "Son of Man" is a better way to speak of Jesus than "Son of God." How would you answer that?*

Answer: "Son of Man" is the most frequently found title for Christ in the New Testament. It occurs over eighty times in the Gospels (I didn't count; I read this somewhere). The title, which originates in Daniel 7:2-14, identifies for Christians the divine origin of Jesus while in a particular way stressing his humanity. In contrast, the term "Son of God" primarily emphasizes Jesus' divinity, without, of course, in any way diminishing his humanity.

An RCIA instructor who states that the former is a "better" title for Jesus than the latter is walking on very thin ice. All the main biblical titles of Jesus (Son of God, Son of Man, Christ, Lord, and so forth) are important in that they bring out different aspects of Christ's person and identity. The various titles complement each other. Playing one off against the others is an entirely unacceptable procedure.

The tendency to diminish the divinity of Jesus is common today in some circles. That such an impulse would make its way into RCIA classes represents a serious pastoral and catechetical problem.

People as Sheep

Question: *I know Jesus often referred to people as sheep. The auxiliary bishop who lives in our parish does it all the time. Does this not suggest that laity are stupid?*

Answer: The biblical symbolism of sheep and shepherds evokes a variety of meanings. Some early iconography portrayed the Twelve Apostles as sheep surrounding Christ the Good Shepherd. Other depictions are of Christ carrying a wounded sheep on his shoulders and of Christ rescuing the wandering lost lamb caught in a bush. Christ himself is venerated as the Lamb of God.

The Twenty-third Psalm contains the best known expression of this imagery: "The Lord is my shepherd; there is nothing I shall want." The essential point is to underscore God's providence, mercy, and love.

Like all images, this one has to be used carefully. Not all the elements of a particular symbol are useful. That sheep are known to be placid and to have high herd instincts is not part of the message about Christ's flock. I assume your auxiliary bishop is careful in his usage. Beginning a homily with the words "My Dear Sheep" would, for instance, probably not go over well.

The World

Question: *Why is John's Gospel negative about the world? Surely the world is good, since it is God's creation.*

Answer: The term "world" has two distinct meanings in biblical and theological language, each of which complements the other. The first meaning is fairly neutral. Here the world is generally identified with the visible universe. This is the created order made by God and subject to his will and providence. As a divine creation, the world is, in this sense, good, not evil.

In the second usage, "world" has a more specific reference: to history as distorted from its true end. There exists the arena of darkness and estrangement from God, the human situation at variance from the divine will. This is what John's Gospel sometimes means by "world"; for instance, when Jesus says in it that he and his disciples "are not of the world" (17:16).

Catholic Christianity is careful to avoid dualistic thinking: that is, the view that the universe is divided equally between good and evil, within an ongoing war between both. Dualism understands the world as simply evil. The authentic Christian perspective is that the world as created and intended by God is good, but that it does have a shadow side of evil, sin, and alienation.

Unforgivable Sin

Question: *If God can forgive all sins, what sense does it make to call something an "unforgivable sin"?*

Answer: The term "unforgivable sin" — or more accurately "blasphemy against the Holy Spirit" — means a fundamental rejection of the possibility of divine forgiveness. The origin of the notion is Matthew, chapter 12. After Jesus had performed a miracle, the Pharisees accused him of using the power of the devil to accomplish the cure. Jesus responded: "Whoever speaks against the Holy Spirit will not be forgiven, either in this age or in the age to come" (Mt 12:32).

Blasphemy against the Holy Spirit is a synonym for spiritual stubbornness. It means a rejection of the gift of forgiveness, because one does not believe in forgiveness or thinks one's sins unforgivable. God cannot force forgiveness on someone who refuses it. However, it is difficult to determine the state of mind of someone with the outlook described here. Only God can judge. God can forgive all sins: but only if we let him.

INRI

Question: *On the top of the crucifix on my rosary are the letters I.N.R.I. and at the bottom is a skull. What do these mean?*

Answer: "I.N.R.I." are the initials of the Latin words "*Iesus Nazarenus, Rex Iudaeorum.*" These letters, often found written above the head of the image of the dead Christ on crucifixes, are the initials for the inscription which Pontius Pilate had placed over the Cross of Christ. The Gospels tell us that Pilate put "Jesus of Nazareth [literally, the Nazarene], King of the Jews" over the Cross and that the words were written in Hebrew, Latin, and Greek (see Mt 27:37; Mk 15:26; Lk 23:38; Jn 19:19-22).

The skull which appears at the bottom of some crucifixes derives from the legend that the hill of Calvary on which Jesus was crucified was the burial place of Adam. Even if this is not historically verifiable, there is still a profound theological meaning here: Jesus is the New Adam who conquers sin and death, overcoming and reversing the history of sin introduced into the world by the original Adam (see 1 Cor 15:45-49; Rom 5:12-21).

Blood and Water

Question: *In a recent homily, I said that Jesus probably died from suffocation due to fluid build-up in the lung area, so that when his side was pierced blood and water flowed out. We can understand the blood, but the water was probably fluid build-up, as modern medicine tells us today. Can you clarify this point for me?*

Answer: The biblical statement that from Jesus' side flowed blood and water is not a coroner's report (see Jn 19:31-34). To explain its significance in the terms you describe is interesting, but it is certainly not what the Scriptures had in mind. That blood and water flowed from the side of Christ was interpreted by early Christian commentators in sacramental terms (see 1 Jn 5:6-8). Christ's death and resurrection are the origin of the sacraments: baptism is signified by the water that flowed from Christ's side, and the Eucharist is symbolized by the blood that issued from the pierced body of the dead Christ.

In any future revision of your homily you may want to curtail the medical analysis and expand on the sacramental meanings that John and the early Christian commentators had in mind.

Who Wrote the Letter to the Hebrews?

Question: *Our parish lector trainer recently told us that St. Paul did not write the Letter to the Hebrews and that we should stop announcing it that way when we read at Mass. Is she right?*

Answer: She is indeed. Now if lectors would only put her teaching into practice! While all lectionaries provide the heading "A Reading from the Letter to the Hebrews," one out of every two lectors (based on my unscientific observations) slips in unwittingly the words "St. Paul to the Hebrews" in the announcement of the reading.

The authorship of the Letter to the Hebrews is not attributed to Paul anywhere in the document itself. Judging by the criteria of style, vocabulary, and thought, scholars have concluded that the Letter was not written by Paul or commissioned by him. The Letter belongs to a world of speech and thought markedly different from the writings of Paul. Even in the early Church, the attribution to Paul did not appear before the late second century. Other well-known persons of the apostolic Church suggested as the authors have included Barnabas and Apollos. The important thing to keep in mind is that, whoever its author, the Letter to the Hebrews is recognized as belonging to the revealed Word of God.

New Jerusalem

Question: *The liturgy talks a lot about Jerusalem, but I am always a little confused on what we are talking about. Help me out.*

Answer: Put simply, the word "Jerusalem" has three references in Catholic Christian understanding. The first is to the actual city of Jerusalem, which was and is central to Jewish life and, of course, to Christianity, since it was there that Christ died and rose again and from there the Church spread throughout the world.

The second reference is to the Church, both to the baptized and to church buildings themselves. Wherever Christ's living Body on earth lives and acts for human salvation, there is Jerusalem. The Catholic rites for the dedication of church buildings are full of references to the Church and church buildings as "Jerusalem."

Third, Jerusalem refers to the heavenly city of the angels and saints. In the Book of Revelation we read: "And I saw the holy city, new Jerusalem, coming down out of heaven from God, prepared as a bride adorned for her husband" (21:2). The New and Eternal Jerusalem is the whole universe of creation, history, and humanity redeemed and glorified in Christ.

The Antichrist

Question: *Where does the number 666 come from in the Bible? Who does it apply to? I have heard it used by some Protestants about the Pope. Who is the antichrist?*

Answer: The infamous number 666 has been applied throughout history to enemies of all kinds: Nero, Hitler, the Pope. The number 666 occurs in the Book of Revelation: "This calls for wisdom: let him who has understanding reckon the number of the beast, for it is a human number, its number is six hundred and sixty-six" (13:18). The number is commonly thought to refer to the antichrist (the one who opposes Christ), because each number represents one less than seven — itself the perfect number. The meaning of this number has given rise to endless speculation, not to mention nonsense.

One (very correct) way to take the wind out of the sails

of 666 enthusiasts and searchers for the antichrist is to point
out that the antichrist is each and every one of us in so far as
we oppose Christ by failing to live up to our baptismal dignity
and our vocations to be virtuous sons and daughters of God.

THREE
Church Structure

Vatican
Church Law
Ecumenism
Pope/Bishop
Religious
Pastoral

Ecumenical Councils

Question: *Where did ecumenical councils come from and how did they develop? Was the Council of Jerusalem the first ecumenical council? When do you think Vatican III will be held?*

Answer: Ecumenical councils (meaning the most formal kind of council for all the bishops of the world) had their general origin in the Council of Jerusalem held in 51 A.D., at which the apostles decided that converts to the Christian faith would not be obliged to observe all the prescriptions of Old Testament law (see Acts of the Apostles, ch. 15).

However, ecumenical councils as such are not dated from that council but from the First Council of Nicaea held in the year 325 (at which the original Nicene Creed was formulated). About 300 bishops participated in that council.

The councils before Nicaea were simple and less formal. As early as the second century, bishops gathered in regional meetings and synods to make decisions for the doctrinal and pastoral good of their local churches. The expansion of such limited assemblies into full-fledged ecumenical councils was a logical evolution to respond to the growing needs of the Church.

When will Vatican III be held? If they elect me pope (which would put me in the only reliable position to answer that question), the answer will be: after my pontificate! While one hears calls from various quarters for another ecumenical council, the need does not appear to be overwhelming at present. Vatican II continues to provide the program of renewal that the Church needs.

My expectation (and hope) is that the next ecumenical council will involve some process of the reunification of Catholicism and Orthodoxy (a project that unfortunately continues to defy the clock!).

Smoke of Satan

Question: *Exactly what was Pope Paul VI referring to when he made the comment in the 1970s that "The smoke of Satan had entered the Church"?*

Answer: Pope Paul VI did make the statement you ascribe to him. This pope had the heavy responsibility of leading the Church through most of Vatican II and implementing its reforms in the years thereafter. He was without doubt a great believer in the council, and without him it would not have had the positive results it did.

However, Paul VI was not oblivious to the distortions and confusions that inevitably attended the Church in the postconciliar period. The Church was not only buffeted externally by the heavy winds of a cultural revolution but by theological controversies, ecclesiastical turmoil, and liturgical and pastoral abuses within the Church itself.

In a more pessimistic moment, Pope Paul interpreted the latter in terms of the "smoke of Satan" entering the Church. A dramatic observation to be sure, but more should not be made of it than the pope intended. Clearly, Pope Paul VI thought that the fire of the Holy Spirit in the post-Vatican II period was always stronger than the smoke of Satan.

Vatican Protocol

Question: *In a recent television program, I noticed how much protocol there is in the Vatican. Is there a book where I could find out more about this?*

Answer: The only popular book of which I am aware is by James-Charles Noonan, Jr., and is titled *The Church Visible: The Ceremonial Life and Protocol of the Roman Catholic Church* (check with your local Catholic bookstore). This work offers detailed analyses of ecclesiastical ceremonies and conventions, vesture and insignia, honors and titles.

A second edition of the book would benefit from correction of the considerable number of technical and factual imprecisions and errors found in the present edition. Some will think that the work suffers from excessive editorializing and that it occasionally lapses from sober judgment. However, the non-specialist reader will find it a useful source of general information. The book is attractively produced and eminently readable.

The Dysfunctional Church

Question: *Recently a speaker gave a lecture in our parish about how dysfunctional the Church is. I was very distressed, but did not know how to answer.*

Answer: I have on my shelves two books on this theme. One is *The Dysfunctional Church* by Michael H. Crosby and the other is *The Codependent Church* by Virginia Curran Hoffman. Should your speaker have been reflecting material from either of these books (which is likely), I can only say that these works would not be described by thoughtful people as learned, profound, or well-balanced.

Codependency and dysfunctionality theory was popular in social work and psychotherapy about a decade ago. The basic argument is that human beings and institutions (marriages, families, churches) are addicted to all kinds of destructive relationships and that all sorts of sicknesses masquerade under the name of helping others, self-sacrifice, and commitment — in short, that the world is basically more screwed up than we ever dreamed!

Respectable psychiatrists and psychologists generally dismiss the sort of theory you mention as medically faddish and superficial, so it can hardly be very useful in looking at the Church. There can be some value in psychological analyses of ecclesiastical institutions, but I wouldn't look for it in pop psychology.

If you want to read an accessible (and very funny) critique of codependency and dysfunctionality theory get hold of Wendy Kaminer's book entitled *I'm Dysfunctional, You're Dysfunctional*.

Canon Law

Question: *What is the Code of Canon Law and where can I get one? Is it for clergy only, or also for lay people? Why does it exist? Where did it come from?*

Answer: Over the centuries, the Church, like most institutional entities, has operated with a body of laws. Church law is not an end in itself but serves the good order of the Church and the vocation to which Christians individually and corporately are called: sanctification in Christ.

As one would expect, ecclesiastical law has varied considerably over the centuries. The first complete and comprehensive modern codification of canon law was issued in 1917.

This code was revised after the Second Vatican Council (1962-65), and the present Code of Canon Law was promulgated by Pope John Paul II on Jan. 25, 1983.

Canon law is not just for clergy but for the whole Church. While Church law is the particular competence of canon lawyers (those trained in ecclesiastical law), anyone can acquire a copy of the code (available from the Canon Law Society of America through Catholic bookstores).

This volume does not make for exciting reading (any more than the manual for your automobile or exercise bicycle), and it takes considerable skill to interpret it correctly;

however, it can serve as a useful educational tool for all
Catholics.

Counter-Reformation

Question: *I was recently reading about the Counter-Reformation. Were there not some good things in the Protestant Reformation? Why would the Church oppose the Reformation so vigorously?*

Answer: By the Counter-Reformation is meant a period of reform in the Catholic Church extending from about 1520 to about 1650. It came into existence not only as a means to stem the tide of Protestantism but to advance genuine reform within the Catholic Church itself.

Important factors of this renewal included the establishment of new religious orders, such as the Society of Jesus (Jesuits) and the restoration of older orders to their original observances — an example being the reform of the Carmelites under St. Teresa of Ávila.

The main agents of the Counter-Reformation were the papacy and the Council of Trent (1545-63). Prominent among Church leaders leading the reform were St. Charles Borromeo, archbishop of Milan, and St. Francis de Sales, bishop of Geneva.

Certainly, there were some good things about the Protestant Reformation: the emphasis on the Word of God, making the liturgy more accessible to the people, seeking to abandon superstitious elements in Christian life.

The Counter-Reformation should not be seen merely as an opposition to the Protestant Reformation, but as a desire in some respects to respond to its legitimate concerns. For this reason, the movement is better (and more accurately) referred to as the Catholic Reformation.

On Lutherans
Question: *How exactly do Catholics and Lutherans differ?*

Answer: An impressive series of dialogues between Lutherans and Catholics worldwide yielded an important common statement on the Eucharist in 1968, and a statement on Eucharist and ministry in 1970. Significant discussions on papal primacy, teaching authority, and infallibility in the Church culminated in joint statements published in 1973 and 1978.

The most thorny question is probably justification: the extent to which Christians cooperate in their own salvation. Martin Luther thought that the Church of his time was paying too much attention to religious practices, such as pilgrimages, fasting, and gaining indulgences, and not enough to the unearned initiative of God's grace. Since the Reformation, Catholics have in turn thought that Lutherans emphasized faith alone in a way that played down the importance of human cooperation with God and rendered believers rather passive.

Considerable strides have been made in achieving the proper balance, leading to a joint (if not unanimous) Lutheran-Catholic statement on justification by faith in 1983. All in all, recent Lutheran-Catholic dialogue has brought both churches closer together than at any time since the Reformation.

Episcopalian Identity
Question: *I don't understand the relationship between Episcopalians and Anglicans. What is the history of the Episcopal Church?*

Answer: "Anglican" is the generic name for the daughter churches of the Church of England established during the English Reformation. Those known as "Anglicans" in

England, Australia, and Canada are called "Episcopalians" in Scotland and the United States. The terms are generally interchangeable.

Anglicanism came to America in 1607 with the Jamestown, Virginia, settlers. In 1783 American Anglicanism became formally known as the Protestant Episcopal Church. At the time American Anglicans declared themselves independent of the Church of England, while remaining in communion with it. They kept their ecclesiastical practices generally in conformity with the Church of England, though they revised the (English) Book of Common Prayer, simplifying and omitting a number of elements.

The Episcopal Church in the United States, like all Anglican churches, belongs to the worldwide Anglican Communion, which has the Archbishop of Canterbury as its titular head.

American Episcopalians reflect the whole spectrum of Anglicanism, ranging from Anglo-Catholic or High churches (those closer to Rome in faith and liturgy) to Low church groups (which are closer to evangelical Protestantism).

Americans who describe themselves as Anglicans generally belong to the High-church end of the spectrum.

Eastern Churches

Question: *I am very confused about the Eastern rites. I can never tell which ones are Catholic and which are not.*

Answer: When I was teaching an undergraduate class on liturgy some years ago, the topic of Eastern rites came up. Upon my describing the liturgies of the East, a puzzled young lady raised her hand and said, "I'm from New Jersey and we don't do any of that there." I had to explain that the Eastern churches are not those of New Jersey and New York (nor are

Utah and Idaho the Western churches). Confusion about Eastern churches is not unusual.

The Eastern churches are those which follow the rites which historically developed in the patriarchates of Constantinople, Alexandria, Antioch, and Jerusalem, just as the liturgies of the West developed from Rome.

Before the eleventh century, most of the Eastern churches were in communion with Rome. Since then, the Eastern churches have been divided between those that are in communion with Rome and those that are not. For churches in communion with Rome, the key word to watch for is "Catholic" (Byzantine Catholic, Ukrainian Catholic). Those churches not in communion with Rome go by the title "Orthodox" (Greek Orthodox, Russian Orthodox). This rule of thumb is not ironclad, but it works most of the time.

Eastern Catholics

Question: *My sister-in-law, a Maronite Catholic, was upset when she visited our parish and the pastor told her he admired "Uniate Catholics." Please explain to me why. Actually, I don't really understand Uniates.*

Answer: The so-called "Uniate churches" are the Eastern Catholic churches who profess the same doctrines as the rest of Catholicism. The liturgical rites, canon law and spirituality of the Eastern Catholic churches vary, however, in many respects from those of the Latin West.

The various communities of Eastern Catholicism originated in the venerable centers of Antioch, Alexandria, and Byzantium. Eastern Catholic clergy are often married. Nearly all of the Orthodox churches possess corresponding "Uniate" groups who acknowledge their allegiance to the pope (although there are no Maronites not in communion with Rome).

The term "Uniate," though found in older historical literature, is rarely used by Eastern Catholics themselves, who feel that it suggests second-class Catholic identity or that they are the "poor relations" in the Catholic family (a feeling for which, unfortunately, there exists some historical grounds). The term "Uniate" is best avoided for that reason.

I wouldn't announce during your sister-in-law's next visit that you "don't really understand Uniates." She might take it personally. You may wish instead to declare an interest in your further education on her tradition and ask her to find you some accessible literature on Maronite Catholicism.

Maronite Catholics

Question: *Are Maronites really Catholics in the full sense? I am not sure where their rites fit in. Why do the different rites exist, and what are they?*

Answer: Maronites are as Catholic as the Pope! One of the sad facts about Latin Catholics is the inadequate knowledge many of us have regarding the existence and status of the Eastern Catholic churches. The *Catechism of the Catholic Church* answers your second question as follows: "The liturgical traditions or rites presently in use in the Church are the Latin (principally the Roman rite, but also the rites of certain local churches, such as the Ambrosian rite, or those of certain religious orders) and the Byzantine, Alexandrian or Coptic, Syriac, Armenian, Maronite, and Chaldean rites" (no. 1203). Vatican II declared that all these rites are of equal dignity and standing in Catholicism.

Why do these rites exist? The *Catechism* provides the answer: "The diverse liturgical traditions have arisen by very reason of the Church's mission. Churches of the same geographical and cultural area came to celebrate the mystery of Christ through particular expressions characterized by the culture. . . . Through the liturgical life of a local church, Christ, the light and salvation of all peoples, is made manifest to the particular people and culture to which that Church is sent and in which she is rooted. The Church is catholic, capable of integrating into her unity, while purifying them, all the authentic riches of cultures" (no. 1202).

Pope's Titles

Question: *I recently read that the Pope is not only the bishop of Rome, but also the archbishop of Rome. Is that correct?*

Answer: Cutting through a lot of theology, history and convention, holy orders in the Church have a tripartite structure: bishop, priest, and deacon. All else is variations on these (canons, monsignors, archbishops, cardinals, patriarchs).

All bishops share episcopal ministry equally (the bishop of Salt Lake City, the archbishop of Denver, the cardinal archbishop of New York, and the pope). The pope's greatest dignity is as bishop of Rome (the greatest dignity of the cardinal archbishop of Manila is that he is bishop of Manila). The Pope is pope precisely because he is bishop of Rome.

However, as bishop of Rome, the pope is head of the college of bishops and thus has a unique role among bishops. It is correct to say that the pope is also metropolitan (or archbishop) of the ecclesiastical province of Rome, as well as primate of Italy (as Cardinal Józef Glemp is primate of Poland). Because he is bishop of Rome, he is also vicar of Christ, patriarch of the West, supreme pontiff, and servant of the servants of God.

However, I would not encourage you to start referring to the pope as archbishop of Rome. People might think you were being eccentric (and they would be right).

Vicariate of Rome

Question: *If the Pope is the bishop of Rome, how does he run his diocese and the whole Catholic Church as well?*

Answer: The diocese of Rome is administered on a day-to-day basis by a cardinal with the title of vicar general for Rome. The vicarate administration is located near the Basilica of St. John Lateran, the cathedral of the diocese of Rome and the mother church of Christendom (even more important, for that reason, than St. Peter's Basilica).

In 1558, Pope Paul IV determined that the vicar of Rome should be a member of the College of Cardinals. In 1929, Pope Pius XI withdrew the Vatican proper from the jurisdiction of the vicar for the city of Rome. There exists today a separate vicar general for Vatican City, who is also the archpriest of St. Peter's Basilica.

Pope John Paul II, like Pope Paul VI before him, pays close attention to the needs of the diocese of Rome, and he regularly visits the parishes of the city and suburbs.

Vicar of Christ

Question: *I thought the Pope is the vicar of Christ. My pastor says all bishops are vicars of Christ. Which is correct? Where did the term come from?*

Answer: Both you and your pastor are correct. "Vicar of Christ" refers to one who takes the place of Christ. The term is appropriately used of the pope and of all bishops.

While the usage of this title derives from the fifth century, the Council of Florence in its Decree for the Greeks (1439) defined the pope as the "true Vicar of Christ." This language was highlighted strongly by the First Vatican Council in 1870. The Second Vatican Council calls bishops in general "vicars and legates of Christ" (*Lumen Gentium*, no. 27), indicating that the title does not apply exclusively to the bishop of Rome.

Vatican II emphasized that all bishops are vicars of Christ for their local churches, as the pope is for the universal church. The title "Vicar of Christ" denotes that bishops receive their power not by delegation of the pope but from Christ himself in virtue of episcopal ordination.

The Church is best seen, not as a multinational corporation with headquarters in Rome, but as a communion of local churches united by the See of Peter. Bishops act not as "branch managers" of the papacy, but perform their office in their own right — always, of course, in communion with the pope.

Papal Pageantry

Question: *Why does the pope no longer wear a crown? What did the old crown mean? I liked the pageantry of the popes when I was young. Why was all this done away with?*

Answer: Much of the papal pageantry familiar to Catholics in the earlier part of the century derived from the era of monarchies. Since monarchial systems collapsed rapidly in the twentieth century, it was necessary for the papacy to detach itself from the symbols of monarchy. Besides, the pope is not a monarch. An additional impetus came from the desire after Vatican II (to borrow a phrase) to advance the "noble simplicity" of the papacy.

The beehive-shaped triple crown formerly worn by popes was a development of the medieval papacy. Symbolic interpretations of its significance abounded, including the triple office of the pope in serving the church militant, suffering, and triumphant.

For centuries, a crowning marked the beginning of a

pontificate. Pope John Paul I dropped this tradition in 1978 when he was invested instead with the pallium (a symbol of the unity of the pope with bishops throughout the world). Pope John Paul II maintained this innovation of his predecessor.

Papal Nuncio

Question: *How does the papal nuncio in a country fit into the hierarchy of the Church? Is he the boss of the U. S. bishops?*

Answer: The papal nuncio is an archbishop representing the pope in the capital of a foreign country. He has two roles. One is to handle affairs between the Vatican and the civil government of the country to which he is assigned. In this role, the nuncio acts as an ambassador. In many Catholic countries, the nuncio is by tradition the dean of the diplomatic corps.

The other role of the nuncio (but by no means the lesser one) is to handle relations between the pope and the bishops of a particular nation. In this role, the appointee represents the Holy See to the local bishops. The best known aspect of this role of a nuncio is to work with the bishops in recommending to the Vatican Congregation for Bishops (and ultimately the pope) candidates for the episcopacy.

The nuncio is not the "boss" of the bishops in the U.S., or elsewhere, but the servant of communion between the pope and the local bishops. His duties do not properly interfere with the jurisdiction of local bishops, but serve rather to strengthen the general condition of the local church.

Where a country does not have formal diplomatic relations with the Holy See (so that the diplomatic role of the papal representative is less pronounced), the title "apostolic delegate" is used.

Catholic Patriarchs

Question: *The Catholic bishop of Jerusalem is called a "patriarch." What does this mean? I thought only the Orthodox Church had patriarchs. Are there other patriarchs in the Catholic Church?*

Answer: Your question opens up a hornet's nest of ecclesiastical and ecumenical complexity that would take pages to deal with. What follows is my "bare bones" answer. In general, a patriarch is a bishop of the highest order of jurisdiction and honor in Eastern and Western Christianity. From ancient times, the pope as bishop of Rome has had the title "Patriarch of the West," clearly fitting the definition of a patriarch. The two better-known patriarchs of present-day Eastern Orthodoxy are the Patriarch of Constantinople and the Patriarch of Moscow.

Two other kinds of patriarchs exist in the Catholic Church: those of Eastern Rite Catholicism and the honorary patriarchies of Latin Rite Catholicism. Eastern Rite Catholic patriarchs include the patriarchs of the Syrians, the Maronites, the Greek Melkites, the Copts, the Chaldeans, and the Armenians. Some regard Eastern Catholic patriarchs as ranking above cardinals.

In present-day Latin Rite Catholicism, the term "patriarch" is (apart from the papal patriarchate) of honorary status. Latin Rite patriarchs today include the archbishops of Lisbon, Venice, Goa (for the East Indies), and the bishop of Jerusalem.

The Powers of Archbishops

Question: *I always thought that archbishops were in charge of bishops. Is this not true?*

Answer: In a word, "no." In the Latin church, dioceses (headed by bishops) are grouped into provinces. The 148 dioceses of the U.S. are divided into 33 provinces. In each province there is one archdiocese (headed by an archbishop, also called the metropolitan). The archbishop of San Antonio, for example, presides over the province of San Antonio (the largest in the country), which includes 14 dioceses within the state of Texas.

An archbishop has no authority over the bishops or dioceses of the province. He is, however, required to be vigilant about the faith and ecclesiastical discipline within the province and to inform the Holy See of significant problems. (Usually the media trump the archbishop in this initiative nowadays!)

The archbishop may perform an official visitation to a diocese if the local bishop has been neglectful — but only with Rome's approval. Meetings of the bishops of a province to discuss and agree upon matters of common interest and concern (such as proposing candidates for the episcopacy and developing common provincial pastoral policies) are presided over by the archbishop. Generally, archbishops are accorded a degree of honor within their provinces. They will often conduct episcopal ordinations and be present for major occasions in the dioceses.

Pallium

Question: *Recently I moved from a small diocese to Chicago and saw the cardinal wear a little white vestment with crosses around his neck. What is the meaning of this item?*

Answer: I assume you are referring to a vestment called the "pallium." The pallium is an inch or so wide, white in color, made of wool, and ornamented with six small black crosses. Two strips attached in front and behind are worn over the chest and back. This vesture is symbolic of the union of archbishops (not just cardinals) with the pope as bishop of Rome (the pope himself wears a pallium). In the Eastern Catholic churches, patriarchs are also given this vestment. Ordinary bishops (and titular archbishops) do not wear the pallium.

The pallium is made from the wool of two lambs blessed in the Church of St. Agnes in Rome on January 21 (the saint's feast day). The palliums (or pallia, if you want to be fussy) are kept in a niche under the main altar of St. Peter's before being given by the pope to new archbishops — according to recent practice yearly — on June 29, the feast of Sts. Peter and Paul.

Coadjutor and Auxiliary Bishops

Question: *What is the difference between an auxiliary and a coadjutor bishop? Can the bishop of the diocese get rid of an auxiliary or coadjutor if he doesn't like them?*

Answer: An auxiliary bishop, while possessing the fullness of episcopal orders, is an assistant to the diocesan bishop (technically called the "Ordinary"). He aids the bishop in the governance of the diocese and can take his place if the latter is absent or impeded. A diocese may have one or more auxiliary bishops depending on the pastoral need (generally signified by the size of the Catholic population).

A coadjutor bishop (of which there can be only one in a diocese) acts effectively like an auxiliary bishop. The major difference is that he possesses the right to succeed the bishop of the diocese upon the retirement or death of the latter, while an auxiliary does not have right of succession.

Coadjutors are often appointed when the diocesan bishop may no longer be able to function at "full throttle," so to speak, but is not yet ready for retirement or when serious problems associated with the diocesan bishop's actions or leadership exist in a diocese.

Bishops of any status are difficult to "get rid of." A bishop who does not like his auxiliary might hope that Rome will promote the latter to head his own diocese (a hope the auxiliary may also nurture!). However, a diocesan bishop is pretty much stuck with his coadjutor.

Thankfully, the dire problem of bishops wanting to get rid of each other is generally prevented by the care with which diocesan bishops and their auxiliaries or coadjutors are matched and (one may piously hope) by the grace that comes with episcopal ordination generally.

Titular Bishops

Question: *Our auxiliary bishop is also the titular bishop of a diocese in Ireland. Can you explain this to me? I'm confused.*

Answer: Every diocese (including archdioceses) can only have one "ordinary" bishop (just like cities can only have one mayor). By tradition, however, bishops who are not "ordinaries," but rather auxiliaries, coadjutors, vicars apostolic, or bishop-officials in the Roman Curia, are assigned to honorary or titular (in title only) dioceses now defunct.

Many of these inoperative sees are in such places as Asia and North Africa. After the Catholic Church was wiped out in these areas, the extinct dioceses were called sees "in the lands of the infidels." In 1882, Pope Leo XIII changed the designation to "titular sees."

Though hardly the land of the infidels (by most reckonings), Ireland has numerous titular sees — the remnants of amalgamations of very small dioceses into larger ones in the middle ages. The present Irish Diocese of Meath, for instance, once had within its present boundaries up of eleven small dioceses.

Your auxiliary bishop is functionally an assistant to the real or "ordinary" bishop of your diocese, but he is the honorary bishop of a diocese that probably went out of existence in the middle ages. A bishop may visit his titular see as a tourist, but he has absolutely no jurisdiction there. For all you know (or he cares), the titular diocese may have been washed into the ocean centuries ago.

Bishop's Crozier

Question: *What is the meaning of the staff that bishops carry? My bishop's staff has a snake at the top of it. Please explain.*

Answer: (I assume the snake is not a live one!) The staff or crozier used by bishops has its origin in the ancient straight scepter which symbolized ruling authority. The earliest reference to the use of the staff by Christian bishops dates from fifth century. In its developed form, the pastoral staff was a rod of wood with a head of metal, probably "crooked" to evoke the role of the bishop as shepherd.

In the middle ages, episcopal staffs became quite elaborate and incorporated a variety of symbolism. The serpent motif in the decor (much more common in Eastern than Western Christianity) refers to the staff of Moses. During the Exodus, Moses carried in his hand "the rod of God" (Ex 17:9). With this staff, he struck the rock from which water flowed to save the thirst-stricken Israelites (Ex 17:1-6; Num 20:1-11). After the plague of serpents, God gave Moses the instruction: " 'Make a fiery serpent, and set it on a pole; and every one who is bitten, when he sees it, shall live' " (Num 21:8).

In John's Gospel, this Old Testament event is interpreted

as a prefigurement of Christ upon the cross as the source of life: "And as Moses lifted up the serpent in the wilderness, so must the Son of man be lifted up, that whoever believes in him may have eternal life " (3:14-15). Episcopal staffs bearing serpent imagery signify the bishop's role as leader of his people under the power of the life-giving cross.

Religious Enclosure

Question: *The one thing I have never understood about orders like the Carmelites and Poor Clares is why they are never allowed to go out of the convent. Please explain why they are enclosed.*

Answer: Enclosure means that in a religious community certain residence areas are reserved for the exclusive use of the members. Generally the stricter forms of enclosure pertain to religious communities of women dedicated to the contemplative life.

The nuns, novices, and postulants live within the confines of the convent. Members may leave the enclosure for medical reasons, for special events (attendance at a papal Mass, for instance), or to found another convent.

Likewise no one enters the cloistered area of the convent except in clearly defined circumstances provided for in ecclesiastical law. For instance, doctors and craftspeople may enter enclosures for professional purposes.

The fundamental notion of enclosure is that one commits oneself to finding God and living out one's life within a boundaried space. One seeks God in the ordinary, the local, the repetitive. Those committed to enclosure make an important statement that spiritually the grass is not always greener on the other side of the hill.

The witness of religious enclosure is important in an

unstable, mobile culture wherein the soul is constantly prone to seeking meaning elsewhere and the mind is dispersed and fragmented by mass media. Enclosed communities remind us that we should seek God where we are and that there exist few circumstances in which holiness may not be sought.

Third Orders

Question: *Do Third Orders exist in the United States? If so, can you explain what they are, describe their membership and give some example?*

Answer: Yes, Third Orders do exist in the United States. These are associations of mostly laymen and laywomen seeking an intense life of faith according to an approved rule "in the world" — that is, outside formal religious communities.

Third Orders are so named to distinguish them from First and Second Orders (to which men and women religious belong, respectively).

Third Orders have their origins in the Middle Ages. St. Francis of Assisi, for instance, founded the Franciscan Third Order (now called Secular Franciscans). Other religious orders followed the same direction, creating in the 15th century the Augustinian, Dominican, Servite, and Carmelite Third Orders.

Members of Third Orders do not wear special dress, and they have everyday modes of employment. The process of becoming a member includes a period of formation, a profession, and a form of vows. Members may recite some portion of the daily Liturgy of the Hours.

Many Catholic parishes have some members who belong to Third Orders. This is particularly true of parishes associated with religious orders. Third Orders play an important role in helping laity acquire a definite spiritual shape for their lives in the midst of family and professional commitments.

Clericalism

Question: *I hear people speak negatively of "clericalism." I don't understand what that means. Today, above any time, we should be supporting our priests.*

Answer: The clergy — meaning bishops, priests, and deacons — are essential to the Church. Their existence derives from Christ's will and the inspiration of the Holy Spirit. I agree that Catholics should support their priests (and the more support the better).

"Isms" of various kinds, however, are by definition distortions or corruptions of realities that in their authentic state are good and necessary.

By "clericalism" I have two things in mind. The first is undue attachment to clerical status and symbolism. For instance, priests who spend too much time or money on clerical garb and vestments or who think clergy deserve preeminence in all social gatherings might be guilty of clericalism.

Clericalism, secondly, is a mode of behavior in which clergy regard themselves as superior to the laity. If there was an old-fashioned version of clericalism, there is also a new-fangled form. This tends to show up in the modern liturgy on a regular basis. When a priest, for instance, improperly changes texts or rites, adapts the liturgy to his tastes, or imposes his personality upon it, then you have a form of "clericalism."

Monsignors

Question: *Our diocese just made a whole group of priests monsignors. Can you explain this title?*

Answer: The title comes from the Italian *monsignore*, which means "my lord." (This monsignor has encouraged his sisters to use the English translation when addressing him, but to no avail!) Archbishops and bishops in Europe are often addressed by this title. It is more commonly used to refer to priests having the titles of "Protonotary Apostolic," "Prelate of Honor" or "Chaplain of Honor." These are honorary distinctions bestowed by the pope on certain priests, usually for distinguished pastoral service or to accompany certain offices (for instance, in the Vatican diplomatic corps). Monsignors are allowed to wear vesture similar to that of a bishop. They are regarded as honorary members of the "papal household." The title carries, however, no intrinsic responsibilities or duties.

Parochial Vicar

Question: *I do not know what the term "parochial vicar" means. I see it in our parish bulletin. Is this a new term?*

Answer: What were formally in the United States called assistant pastors or (in the more egalitarian 1960s and 1970s) associate pastors are today referred to as parochial vicars. This term was chosen for the 1984 Code of Canon Law because it reflects the role of additional priests assigned to parishes as true cooperators with the pastor and not just his servants.

The Code of Canon Law states: "Parochial vicars are priests who render their services in pastoral ministry as co-workers with the pastor in common counsel and endeavor with him and also under his authority" (Canon 545).

Personally, I find the term parochial vicar more trouble than it's worth. You're not alone in being confused about its meaning. Assistant or associate pastor is much clearer and easier to explain. But then they didn't ask me when they wrote the new Code of Canon Law!

The title parochial vicar is here to stay, and with time it will become more familiar to Catholics.

Priests by First Name

Questions: My pastor constantly insists that people call him by his first name and not as "Father." As a "little old lady," I am irritated by this. Please explain the rules of address. What should I do?

Answer: I am all for calling people by their formal titles. We live in a world of over-familiarity which does not breed respect. A traditional rule of thumb is that people address those they are encountering for the first time, as well as people older than themselves, by formal titles until invited to do otherwise.

Public officials (governors, mayors), ecclesiastical leaders (bishops, priests), persons with whom one has a professional relationship (physicians, dentists) are also addressed by their formal titles. But all of this is up for grabs nowadays.

Why your pastor does not wish to be called "Father" I can only surmise. That he "constantly insists" seems excessive. Your desire to avoid calling him by his first name has solid grounding in ecclesiastical tradition. You can't call him nothing, so here's my suggestion: Call him "dear" ("Dear, can I speak to you for a moment?" "That was a nice sermon, dear"). If he responds (as he might), "I'm not 'dear'!" You can respond nicely "Oh, but I think you are!" As a "little old lady" (your own self-description), you will probably get away with this.

Basilica

Question: *What is a basilica? Is a basilica more important than a cathedral?*

Answer: One of my priest friends says that a basilica is a church that has been made a monsignor! Basilica is a title assigned to certain churches because of their antiquity, dignity, historical importance, or significance as centers of worship or pilgrimage. Basilicas may be either major or minor.

The most famous major basilicas are in Rome: St. John Lateran (the pope's cathedral), St. Peter's, St. Paul Outside the Walls, and St. Mary Major. There are also three minor basilicas in Rome.

In the U.S. there are 45 minor basilicas, the best known being the Basilica of the National Shrine of the Immaculate Conception in Washington, D.C.

Sometimes cathedrals are also basilicas, but usually they are not. While a basilica is an honorary designation, a cathedral is the seat of a diocesan bishop. In that sense, cathedrals outrank basilicas both practically and symbolically. One might say that a cathedral is a church that has been made a bishop!

National Parishes

Question: *What is a "national parish"? How does it differ from a regular parish? Are such parishes on the way out?*

Answer: While parishes are normally territorial units, special parishes have been established for persons of specific national or ethnic backgrounds. National parishes were common in the eastern and midwestern cities of the U.S. in the last century and the first part of the twentieth.

Since the 1960s many of the ethnic groups who made up the membership of national parishes have been assimilated into the general population, joining "mainstream" parishes.

When national parishes no longer serve people of the original nationality, they can experience a crisis of purpose.

For that reason, they are often closed down or amalgamated with other parishes.

In recent decades new forms of ministry have arisen to serve the growing African American, Native American, Vietnamese, and Hispanic Catholic populations. Some would argue that separate ethnic or national parishes for such groups are a divisive influence in the Church. I would answer that this need not be so. Ethnic parishes can ensure that systematic and comprehensive ministry to particular Catholic populations is adequately set in place and maintained.

Congregationalism

Question: *My pastor keeps saying that the Catholic Church is not a congregational church. What does he mean? He often says this at heated parish council meetings. He can be quite stubborn and won't listen to anyone.*

Answer: Congregational churches are those in which authority is vested in the congregation and not in the pastor or an outside authority. Congregationalist communities seek to follow democratic principles and procedures in church government (though this intention is often easier proposed than actualized).

In the congregational outlook, all the baptized are ministers of God. No one, therefore, may claim to have any special powers that others do not possess. The right to govern, preach, or lead worship is delegated to an individual by the congregation.

Clearly, Catholicism is not organized congregationally. There exists a definite distinction between the priesthood of the baptized and of the ordained. Those who lead in the Church do so by virtue of sacramental ordination.

I assume that a "heated parish council meeting" is not one held in a room with poor air conditioning! The fact that the Catholic Church is not congregationalist should never be used as a cover for the tendencies of some pastors to disregard the roles of the laity, excuse themselves from appropriate pastoral collaboration, ignore the need for accountability to their people, or play down the importance of substantial consultative processes.

Parish or Community?

Question: *Our pastor says we are not a "parish" but a "Catholic community." All our letterheads and signs now show this change. Please comment.*

Answer: It is not uncommon these days to see "St. Mildred's Parish" changed to "St. Mildred's Catholic Community." As I understand the logic, "parish" has an old-fashioned ring to it, while "Catholic community" has a warmer and more personal tone.

The desire to build up the communal features of the congregation — in itself commendable — is generally the motivation for such name changes. There is, however, a potential problem here.

Historically, a parish is a territorial entity; this means that everything that goes on within the parochial boundaries is the concern of the church. The pastor's responsibility is to all the people within the parish — not just to the "Catholic community." This is why pastors go to Rotary Club, complain about housing to the mayor, and provide invocations for firefighter conventions.

"Parish" is actually a wider and more inclusive term than "Catholic community." Properly, priests and people should have a sense of responsibility for every person, every institution, and every public issue within the parish boundaries. I wouldn't dump the term "parish" yet.

FOUR

Sacraments

Baptism
Confirmation
Eucharist
Reconciliation
Anointing of the Sick
Marriage
Holy Orders

Sponsors and Godparents

Question: *Can two women or two men be sponsors at the baptism of an infant? If not, why not?*

Answer: The Code of Canon Law states that in the matter of baptism, "Only one male or one female sponsor or one of each sex is to be employed" (Canon 873). The logic here is that "sponsor" in the situation of infant baptism (though not necessarily in the case of adult initiation) means "godparent." Just as an infant can have only one natural mother and one natural father, so one can have only one godmother and one godfather at baptism (though only one or the other is required). Clearly Canon Law desires to preserve the gender symbolism of parenthood here.

In a situation in which two men or two women want to be sponsors, the solution would be to have one act as the official sponsor and the other as a witness. The protocol for this is found in Canon Law, which states: "A baptized person who belongs to a non-Catholic ecclesial community may not be admitted except as a witness to baptism and together with a Catholic sponsor" (Canon 874). If a non-Catholic can be a Christian witness at a baptism, then, one supposes, so may a Catholic.

Immersion Fonts

Question: *How does an immersion baptismal font with running water sound to you? Is there a precedent for this? I think it would be a terrible distraction from the sacrament and be very impractical.*

Answer: As a pastor whose church has an immersion baptismal font with running water (although the water does not run all the time), I can attest to the value of an ample font with plenty of water. Precedent is found in the practice of the first centuries of Christianity in which adults were baptized by immersion: that is, by standing or kneeling in the font, with water poured over their heads by the bishop. Immersion is to be distinguished from submersion (that is going under the water), a minority practice in early Christianity.

The 1986 National Statutes for the Catechumenate approved by the U.S. Catholic bishops state: "Baptism by immersion is the fuller and more expressive sign of the sacrament and, therefore, is preferred" (no. 17).

Baptism from a little font ("the old-fashioned way") may be more practical and less distracting, but it is surely not as expressive of the many rich meanings of baptism that include: second birth, crossing over from slavery to freedom, going down into the waters of death, rising with Christ to new life.

Baptism is not a mere technical procedure to be conducted as efficiently and simply as possible (like getting a flu shot). It is a rich and expressive encounter with the great mysteries of faith. An ample font with plenty of water (flowing where possible) serves well the many meanings of baptism.

Mormon Baptism

Question: *Is Mormon baptism valid? Are Mormons Christians?*

Answer: As regards the first question, the official outlook of the Catholic Church up to recently has been inconclusive, as the pronouncements of the various Vatican congregations (departments) over the years indicated. Mormonism is a quite unique strand within Christian history and its baptismal theory has been a challenge for theologians to figure out. Given the prevailing lack of clarity over the years, Mormons were baptized conditionally when received into the Catholic Church.

In 2001, the Vatican Congregation for the Doctrine of the Faith declared decisively that Mormon baptism is not valid. This means that from now on, Mormons will be baptized absolutely when being received into the Catholic Church.

Are Mormons Christians? Since Mormons describe themselves as Christians and seek to follow Christ faithfully, baptismal invalidity does not deprive them of the title "Christian" in a general moral sense. The Vatican declaration was careful to point out that no adverse judgment was being made on the members of the Church of Jesus Christ of Latter-day Saints, and that Catholics and Mormons should continue to work together for the common good.

"Blessing" of a Baby

Question: *My daughter who is not churchgoing does not want her baby baptized until he is older, but only "blessed" (as is done in some churches). Is that possible? Should I ask my pastor about this?*

Answer: While the baptism of infants some weeks after birth is the normative and preferred practice of the Church, an official rite is provided called "Order for the Blessing of a Child Not Yet Baptized." This rite should not be confused with baptism. Its use on an occasion such as you describe might provide an opportunity to catechize the mother on the importance of baptism. If your daughter is willing to have the baby "blessed" by your pastor and he knows the general situation and handles it with sensitivity and pastoral astuteness, then the likelihood of the mother having the child baptized sooner rather than later might be advanced.

Unbaptized Babies

Question: *At the funeral of an unbaptized baby, one of our friends said publicly that the baby will not go to heaven. Everyone was upset. Please comment.*

Answer: Your friend appears to possess excessive theological certainty, plus a poor sense of occasion and timing. On this matter, the *Catechism of the Catholic Church* declares: "As regards *children who have died without Baptism*, the Church can only entrust them to the mercy of God, as she does in her funeral rites for them. Indeed, the great mercy of God who desires that all men should be saved, and Jesus' tenderness toward children which caused him to say: 'Let the children come to me, do not hinder them,' allow us to hope that there is a way of salvation for children who have died without Baptism" (no. 1261). Elsewhere the *Catechism* states: "*God has bound salvation to the sacrament of Baptism, but he himself is not bound by his sacraments*" (no. 1257).

Baptism by Blood, Desire

Questions: *Does the Church still believe in baptism of blood and baptism of desire? If so, can you explain these in updated terms.*

Answer: I'll do my best. The term "baptism of blood" derives from the period during the first three centuries when catechumens or pagans who suddenly converted to the Christian faith but were not yet baptized were put to death. Their death was said to be their baptism.

Baptism of desire means that a person will be saved if, without ever knowing Christ or encountering the Gospel, he or she seeks to live morally and justly. Such a person implicitly "desires" baptism.

The Constitution on the Church of Vatican II stated in this regard: "Those who, through no fault of their own, do not know the Gospel of Christ or his Church, but who nevertheless seek God with a sincere heart, and, moved by grace, try in their actions to do his will as they know it through the dictates of their conscience — those too may achieve eternal salvation" (no. 16).

Baptism in the Spirit

Question: *What is meant by the Baptism in the Spirit? How does this relate to water baptism and to Confirmation?*

Answer: Baptism in the Spirit is the sacrament of water baptism. Period. In Christian history, the tendency to separate water baptism from baptism in the Spirit has recurred on a regular basis. No such distinction is theologically valid. To be baptized by water into Christ is intrinsically to be baptized into the Spirit — who is always the Spirit of Christ.

To the degree that one is baptized into Christ, to that degree one is baptized into the Spirit. To have the gift of the Spirit is to be in Christ. One cannot be in Christ and not have the Spirit.

In evangelical and charismatic Protestantism, a separation between water baptism and a later outpouring of the Spirit has often been made. This found its way somewhat into the Catholic charismatic movement after Vatican II, though it has generally been kept in check.

The only sense in which one can speak of a second baptism in the Spirit is to assert that a moment may come when the meaning and power of one's original water baptism comes to expression in a moment of intense personal conversion.

Confirmation is no more a sacrament of the Spirit or an

outpouring of the Spirit than is baptism. Indeed, all sacraments are sacraments of the Spirit. To say that Confirmation is baptism in the Spirit is not valid in the Catholic scheme of things. The gift of the Spirit received in baptism is deepened, augmented, and sealed in Confirmation. By the same token, Confirmation is a perfection of one's spirit-filled incorporation in Christ through water baptism.

Confirmation Name

Question: *I am an adult recently confirmed at the Easter Vigil. When I asked about choosing a confirmation name at my parish, I was told that the practice is discouraged. What is the history of this practice?*

Answer: Adopting a new name at baptism, Confirmation, or religious profession has a long and varied history. Essentially the practice recognizes that one's name is a crucial aspect of personal identity. Converts to Christianity in the early centuries took the names of saints or martyrs as a way of marking a transition from paganism to Christianity. Eventually the practice was extended to Confirmation and religious profession.

The revised Rite of Baptism of children incorporates the naming of a child. The current Rite of Christian Initiation of Adults provides for adult catechumens choosing a baptismal name when they enter the order of catechumens or during the Preparation Rites on Holy Saturday.

With the modern liturgical renewal came the desire to see Confirmation in close relationship to baptism, so that Confirmation is regarded in some ways as an extension of baptism. Insofar as baptism is an augmentation of Confirmation, candidates implicitly renew their commitment to their baptismal name. The 1971 Rite of Confirmation does not mention the use of a special name at all. However, picking a Confirmation name is, in my opinion, perfectly fine, and no pastor or catechist appropriately forbids or even discourages the practice.

Naming "Confession"

Question: *What is the correct name for what we used to call "Confession"? I was told this name is now incorrect and that the proper name is the "Sacrament of Reconciliation." What is your view?*

Answer: My view is that it is not productive to get hung up on the various names appropriate to the sacrament in question. The *Catechism of the Catholic Church* handles this matter very nicely (nos. 1423-1424), indicating that the sacrament has many "correct" names.

The sacrament is called the "sacrament of conversion" because it makes present Jesus' call to conversion and the Christian's response. It is referred to as the "sacrament of Penance" since it consecrates the Christian process of penance and ongoing renewal of life. It is named the "sacrament of confession" since the act of confession is an essential element of the sacrament. The title "sacrament of forgiveness" is used since by this rite God grants pardon and peace. The sacrament is a "sacrament of Reconciliation" since it draws the sinner into God's reconciling love and restores him or her to the communion of the Church.

The different names bring out different meanings and aspects of the sacrament. These should be used to complement each other, not played off oppositionally.

Frequency of Confession

Question: *The older I get, the more difficult it is for me to* *attend the Sacrament of Confession. Now I confess at least once a year. Is that sufficient?*

Answer: Confession is the only sacrament that does not have its own built-in calendar. Baptism, confirmation, holy orders, and matrimony are "once only" sacraments. Mass is required of all Catholics weekly. The anointing of the sick follows the natural cycles of illness, so that one may receive the sacrament once during a serious illness or when a relapse or a new illness occurs.

Regarding the obligation for confession, the Code of Canon Law states: "After having attained the age of discretion, each of the faithful is bound by an obligation faithfully to confess serious sins at least once a year" (Canon 989). This is the minimal requirement. It applies, however, only to those in serious (or mortal) sin.

Yet, all the canons in the Code that deal with the matter of how often one should have recourse to confession (Canons 246, 276, 664, 719) use the word "frequently." The sacrament is highly recommended in all Church documents, and markedly so in the writings of Pope John Paul II.

How frequent is "frequently"? The Church supplies no answer here. In the "old days," monthly confession was common. A good rule is: one should not go so often that scrupulosity or mere thoughtless routine sets in; by the same token, one should not go so infrequently that confession falls from one's spiritual consciousness.

It seems wise that people consciously construct their own calendars on this matter and faithfully follow them. Going to confession during Advent and Lent is most appropriate. One could add to this the Saturday before the following: one's birthday or baptismal day, the feast of a patron or favorite saint, the feast of one's parish church, or the anniversary of marriage.

Uncertain Confession

Question: *I can no longer use the confessional because I cannot hear the priest's words. I only know he gives me absolution because he makes the Sign of the Cross. I go to my seat and say five Our Fathers, five Hail Marys, and five Glory Be's. I worry about whether I am doing the right thing.*

Answer: You shouldn't worry about your hearing difficulty in going to confession. Your sincere desire to receive the sacrament is what counts. God knows the desires and intentions of your heart.

It would be quite reasonable to bring to confession a piece of paper and a pen and to ask the priest to write out your penance. If the priest doesn't oblige in this matter, then I think your practice of coming up with your own penance is reasonable.

It is always useful at the outset to tell a confessor that you have hearing problems. Most priests in those circumstances do not give complicated penances, but probably something along the lines of what you are devising on your own. Some churches have in their confessionals devices for the hearing-impaired. You could also have someone contact your diocesan chancery or pastoral center and ask about ministry to the deaf in your area.

What to Confess

Question: *I went to confession recently, telling the priest I had no sins from the previous week, but I wanted to confess a sin from my more distant past. The priest told me he could not give me absolution if I hadn't committed any sins. I was taught that confession wasn't just for sinners, but also for people in a state of grace. Has this teaching changed?*

Answer: No one should feel one owes confessors an apology for not having committed sins! You are correct in thinking that confession is not only for serious sins, but also for growth in virtue and holiness.

The introduction to the 1973 Rite of Penance states that "frequent and careful celebration of this sacrament" is very useful as a means of enabling "a serious striving to perfect the grace of baptism" so that the life of Christ "may be seen in us ever more clearly" (no. 7). The numerous papal exhortations of Pope John Paul II on the importance of confession underline this value of the sacrament. What has traditionally been called "confession of devotion" is still entirely valid.

Perhaps the confessor misunderstood your true outlook. If people were to come into confession and tell me they have no sins from the previous week, I would be inclined to think that they may have a somewhat low standard of virtue.

Not a day goes by but all of us are guilty of numerous sins of omission, of failing to do all kinds of good things. Instead of repeating a sin from your distant past, you might more profitably call to mind the failures and missed opportunities of the past week. When one examines one's conscience in this light, there is no shortage of matters to confess.

General Absolution

Question: *Communal penance services with general absolution have become a longstanding tradition in our area. Those who go do not seem to be aware of any requirement for subsequent private confession of serious sins. Please comment.*

Answer: Communal penance services with general absolution are designed for extraordinary situations in which large numbers of people show up for the sacrament, an adequate number of confessors is for genuine reasons unavailable, and the people would otherwise be deprived of the sacrament for a long time (see Code of Canon Law, no. 961). Generally, the conditions for the use of general absolution do not exist in the United States.

You are right in pointing to the requirement that a person who has had serious sins remitted by general absolution must go to individual confession as soon as there is an opportunity to do so (see no. 963).

Is the requirement of subsequent individual confession merely legalistic? No. Individual confession stands at the heart of the Sacrament of Penance. General absolution is a stopgap measure.

It is a bit like a doctor at the end of the day going into the waiting room and telling the remaining patients that he cannot see them individually now, quickly checking each one, giving them something to tide them over, and asking them to come back again.

While general absolution does forgive sins, personal follow-up is necessary for true healing of the soul. Regarding the confession of sins, St. Jerome said, "The medicine cannot heal what it does not know."

Children at Confession

Question: *If only people in mortal sin are required to go to confession, why are children who are preparing for first Communion required to go?*

Answer: You observe correctly that confession — while it is highly commended to all Catholics — is only strictly required of those in mortal sin. Some people might then assume that the Church is saying that all seven-year-olds preparing for first Communion are little mortal sinners. The Church, however, implies no such thing.

The reason for children going to first confession before first Communion was succinctly set out in a 1986 communication to the U.S. bishops from the Vatican Congregation for Divine Worship and the Discipline of the Sacraments, which reads as follows:

"The basis for this observance, for children, is not so much the state of sin in which they may be ... [but] to educate them, from a tender age, to the true Christian spirit of penance and conversion, to growth in self-knowledge and self-control, to the just sense of sin, even of venial sin, to the necessity of asking for pardon of God and, above all, to a loving and confident abandonment to the mercy of the Lord."

In short, the Church asks that children be formally introduced to confession before receiving first Communion so that they will become familiar with the sacrament at an early age and grow accustomed to its frequent usage.

Unforgiven Sin?

Question: *I recently confessed what I consider a fairly grave sin from my preteen years. The priest told me I was too young to have known any better, but I know in my heart that I did. Was my sin absolved even though the priest didn't acknowledge it as a sin? Or do I have to make another confession?*

Answer: As long as you sincerely confessed your sin, you have nothing to worry about. Priests obviously cannot and do not absolve from what are not real sins (missing Sunday Mass through no fault of one's own, for instance). A confessor wisely instructs people to recognize what is objectively sinful and what is not.

You say that you think your sin early was "fairly grave." You deserve the benefit of the doubt here. Whether or not the priest was properly performing his ministry of absolution on behalf of the Church is another question. In any case, you do not need to confess the sin again. Your intention to confess in the first place is the crucial factor here.

No Mortal Sins?

Question: *In a Catholic discussion group I attend, it was proposed that it is no longer necessary to confess a mortal sin. Is this true? It seems that nothing is a sin anymore.*

Answer: Look up the word "sin" in the subject index of the *Catechism of the Catholic Church* and you will find 88 entries (some involving numerous paragraphs). I am not aware of a single sin that has been downgraded in Catholic moral theology since Vatican II. The distinction between mortal and venial sins also remains in operation (see nos. 1854-1864).

What about the requirement to confess mortal sins? Unabashedly quoting the Council of Trent, the new *Catechism* states: "All mortal sins of which penitents after a diligent self-examination are conscious of must be recounted by them in confession" (no. 1456).

Propose to your study group that they take up these sections of the *Catechism* on sin and penance.

Becoming a Catholic Again

Question: *If a Catholic who joined the Mormon church would like to become a Catholic again, what does he need to do? I know someone who is afraid to approach his parish about this.*

Answer: Catholics who formally join another church have placed themselves in a situation of self-imposed excommunication. While such Catholics are no longer in full communion with the church, their Catholic baptism is not and cannot be abrogated.

One who wishes to return to the Catholic Church should approach his or her local pastor to discuss the matter and seek reconciliation with the Church. Pastors are required by pastoral charity to handle these situations with kindness and sensitivity, without playing down the seriousness of the matter. In other words, cranky priests should be avoided!

The priest usually absolves from the "sin of breaking communion" in the absolution provided in the sacrament of Penance and Reconciliation. If the person has been away from the Catholic Church for some time, a period of religious instruction, spiritual direction, and reorientation may be necessary.

General Confession

Question: *Our pastor says we should all make a general confession once in a while. If our sins are forgiven, why should we bring them up again?*

Answer: General confession means a private confession in which the penitent confesses to the priest not only sins actually committed since the last confession, but all past sins, of any magnitude. (This is not the same thing as general absolution.) This practice is traditionally advocated when a person is making a major transition in life, such as entering the priesthood, religious life, or marriage. Some religious communities ask their members to undertake a general confession annually.

Why is this a worthwhile practice? Simply because confession is, as they say, "good for the soul." Confession is not merely a legal procedure (like paying a parking fine), but is medicine for the soul.

Catholics in the Middle Ages had a particularly strong conviction of the value of confession in building up a virtuous life. There are even stories of medieval knights confessing their sins to their horses when no priest was available. (I'm not making this up.)

God of course always knows our sins. What general confession does is help us retain the larger and longer picture of our spiritual lives. God may have long ago forgiven our sins, but their residual effects and the underlying motivations for particular sins may by no means have disappeared from our lives.

Communion in the Hand

Question: *I know the practice is optional, but where did Communion in the hand come from? Don't you think it encourages disrespect?*

Answer: Communion in the hand was the norm for most of the first millennium. Because of the dangers of misuse and the growing concern for reverence, the practice of giving the Host on the tongue was introduced about the ninth century.

The present practice of giving communion in the hand dates from 1969, when Pope Paul VI opened the way for episcopal conferences who wished to reintroduce the practice. Permission was granted to the U.S. bishops in 1977.

In my opinion, there is nothing intrinsically more reverent about reception on the tongue or less reverent about receiving in the hand. Reverence or irreverence are generally determined by other factors: the spiritual attitude of the recipient, the demeanor of the one giving communion, the adequacy of eucharistic understanding, and the manner in which the eucharistic elements are treated both within and outside Mass.

St. Cyril of Jerusalem in the fourth century offered a powerful catechesis on the mode of receiving communion in the hand that is still applicable today: "When you approach, do not go stretching out your open hands or having your fingers spread out, but make the left hand into a throne for the right which shall receive the King, and then cup your open hand and the Body of Christ, reciting the 'Amen.' Then sanctify with all care your eyes by touching the Sacred Body, and receive it. But be careful that no particles fall, for what you lose would be to you as if you had lost some of your members. Tell me, if anybody had given you gold dust, would you not hold fast to it with all care, and watch lest some of it fall and be lost to you? Must you not then be even more careful with that which is more precious than gold and diamonds, so that no particles are lost?"

Lutherans and Real Presence

Question: *Do Lutherans believe in the Real Presence? I thought all Protestants reject the idea that Christ is present in the Eucharist.*

Answer: First of all, there is a great variety of Protestant theologies of Christ's eucharistic presence. Among "high church" Anglicans, for instance, some hold views very close to those of Catholicism, while the "low church" or evangelical wing stands at some distance from Catholic belief.

Lutheran eucharistic theology is quite close to Catholic faith in some respects. The 1978 Lutheran-Roman Catholic Final Report on the Eucharist states: "Roman Catholic and Lutheran Christians together confess the real and true presence of the Lord in the Eucharist. There are differences, however, in theological statements on the mode and therefore duration of the real presence."

The Report continues: "The Roman Catholic Church teaches that 'Christ whole and entire' becomes present through the transformation of the whole substance of the bread and the wine into the substance of the body and blood of Christ while the empirically accessible appearances of bread and wine (*accidentia*) continue to exist unchanged. This 'wonderful and singular change is most aptly called "transubstantiation" by the Catholic Church.' "

Lutherans, the same document points out, "have given expression to the reality of the eucharistic presence by speaking of a presence of Christ's body and blood in, with, and under bread and wine — but not of transubstantiation."

Nevertheless, "The Lutheran tradition affirms the Catholic tradition that the consecrated elements do not simply remain bread and wine but rather by the power of the creative word are given as the body and blood of Christ. In this sense Lutherans also could occasionally speak, as does the Greek tradition, of a 'change.' "

Eucharist as Symbol
Question: *In a Lenten series in our parish, the speaker referred often to the Eucharist as a symbol. Isn't this a Protestant approach?*

Answer: It certainly could be, depending on the way in which the word "symbol" is being used regarding the Eucharist.

If by symbol is meant something that reminds us of another reality or something that sparks our imagination (a butterfly is a symbol of the resurrection; the Church is symbolized by a ship), then a very weak theory of symbol is at work here. To speak of the Eucharist as symbol in this manner would be entirely inadequate.

But there are also strong theories of symbolism (a

ceasefire agreement effects a ceasefire; giving food to the hungry symbolizes care for the poor). This understanding of symbol is much more aptly applied to the Eucharist. To say that Christ is symbolically present in the Eucharist is to say that the tangible realities of bread and wine become the means by which Christ is really and truly present.

All in all, however, the word symbol as popularly understood is too vague and misleading to be applied to eucharistic presence. For this reason it is better avoided.

Bread and Wine

Question: *In my parish my fellow eucharistic ministers talk of the "bread" and the "wine" and never of the "Body" and "Blood" of Christ. Comment.*

Answer: Eucharistic ministers are at least required to use the words "The Body of Christ" and "The Blood of Christ" when distributing the eucharistic elements at Mass. Apart from these occasions, a variety of terms may be used: the "host" and the "cup," "eucharistic bread" and "eucharistic wine," "consecrated bread" and "consecrated wine."

Some argue that the use of the simple words "bread" and "wine" is improper. This argument, in my opinion, should not be pushed too far. These unadorned terms appear, in fact, in the official liturgical books themselves, including in the eucharistic prayer. But the meaning they have in those contexts is that of Catholic eucharistic doctrine.

There exists a danger that in using the terms "bread" and "wine" exclusively or normatively, Catholic belief in the Real Presence will be lost sight of or neglected. For this reason, I think it wise that words other than "bread" and "wine" be used, especially in catechesis and sacramental preparation — and not least with children.

Eucharistic ministers should give good example in this matter.

Fasting Before Communion

Question: *I am confused about the rules of fasting before Mass. Why do we fast before receiving Communion?*

Answer: The Code of Canon Law sets out the current regulation: "One who is to receive the Most Holy Eucharist is to abstain from any food or drink, with the exception only of water and medicine, for at least the period of one hour before Holy Communion" (Canon 919, par. 1). However, there are exceptions: "Those who are advanced in age or who suffer from any infirmity, as well as those who take care of them, can receive the Most Holy Eucharist even if they have taken something during the previous hour" (par. 3).

There are many meanings and purposes to the practice of fasting before eucharistic reception, among them the need for Catholics to approach the Eucharist in a physically and spiritually concentrated fashion. Fasting also reminds us of the great difference between earthly food, which sustains only perishable life, and the food of the Eucharist, which is the medicine of immortality.

At Communion, May I Only Say "Amen"?

Question: *When I converted to Catholicism in 1964, I was taught that, at Communion, we could say "Jesus," "Master" or whatever was meaningful to us in response to "the Body of Christ." But my associate pastor told me that there is only one correct response: "Amen." I would like your input.*

Answer: I hope your associate pastor was very nice to you when he did so. It's not as if you were publicly proclaiming heresy! While the formula for the distribution and reception of Communion has varied over the centuries, the standard response is simply "Amen." It is possible that you were caught in the crossfire of a transitional moment, thus catechized in the manner you describe.

The present dialogue between the one distributing and the one receiving Communion derives, generally speaking, from the fourth century. The response "Amen" is a rich, all-inclusive affirmation that incorporates the words you yourself have been saying. "Amen" means "truly," "so be it," "I believe." By saying "Amen," you would be publicly expressing your assent with the whole Church, not making a response that is merely private or personal.

Precious Blood to the Sick

Question: *In my parish, some eucharistic ministers are bringing the consecrated wine to the sick. I never heard of this. Is this allowed?*

Answer: Yes, but it is rare. The 1972 Rite of Anointing and Pastoral Care of the Sick states: "A sick person who is unable to receive the eucharist under the form of bread may receive communion under the form of wine alone" (no. 46). Later, it says: "The precious blood should be carried in a vessel which is closed in such a way as to eliminate all danger of spilling." If some of the precious blood remains, "it should be consumed by the minister; he will also wash the vessel" (no. 95).

This method of Communion requires the greatest of care. Understandably, some bishops and pastors are reluctant to approve it in their dioceses and parishes. However, this practice is "on the books," so to speak, and is therefore legitimate.

Eucharistic Cannibalism

Question: *Non-Catholics and Catholics I know say if we believe in the true eucharistic presence of Christ as Body and Blood, we are like cannibals when we receive Communion.*

Answer: It is understandable that (through misinformation) some non-Catholics might think that Catholics hold a cannibalistic understanding of the Eucharist. However, that Catholics themselves would think this is surprising, and it indicates a serious lack of an adequate understanding of eucharistic presence.

The charge of eucharistic cannibalism has been made from the earliest days of Christianity. The Church has always refuted the notion by insisting that "body" and "blood" in the Eucharist do not correspond to actual meat and blood as we understand these in everyday life. This is why the Church has always been skeptical of stories of "bleeding hosts," of images of Christ crucified appearing in the host, or of bread that turns into flesh after the consecration.

To hold that believers receive in the Eucharist the body and blood of Christ is to say that by the power of the Spirit the bread and wine, while remaining in appearance bread and wine, are changed into the very being of the risen and glorified Christ. This is in no way to play down the Real Presence of Christ in the Eucharist. In the Eucharist we receive nothing less than the whole person of the risen Christ.

The Church's doctrine of transubstantiation excludes the idea that Christ's body and blood are cannibalized in eucharistic communion.

Viaticum

Question: *When I was young the term "Viaticum" was used for Communion to the dying. Do we still use that term?*

Answer: The term "Viaticum" is indeed still used. It means "food for the journey" and refers to the reception of Communion when death is imminent.

The *Catechism of the Catholic Church* states: "As the sacrament of Christ's Passover the Eucharist should always be the last sacrament of the earthly journey, the 'viaticum' for 'passing over' to eternal life" (no. 1517).

The *Catechism* continues: "Communion in the body and blood of Christ, received at this moment of 'passing over' to the Father, has a particular significance and importance. It is the seed of eternal life and the power of resurrection, according to the words of the Lord: 'He who eats my flesh and drinks my blood has eternal life, and I will raise him up at the last day' [Jn 6:54]. The sacrament of Christ once dead and now risen, the Eucharist is here the sacrament of passing over from death to life, from this world to the Father" (no. 1524).

Spiritual Communion

Question: *On the Masses broadcast daily on EWTN, the commentator often speaks of "Spiritual Communion." I don't fully understand what that means. Please explain.*

Answer: Spiritual Communion is traditionally understood as the fervent desire to receive the Eucharist. This attitude should habitually precede the reception of the sacrament. Spiritual Communion is also expressed in attitudes of faith and love throughout the day after one has received the Eucharist. To receive Communion "in spirit" means that the fruits of the sacrament overflow into charity, a more profound faith, and deeper devotion to Christ.

The act of receiving Communion should never be merely external or routine, but must penetrate the heart and mind.

Otherwise its graces are not realized in the worshiper.

Spiritual Communion may also be practiced by those who are unable to approach the Eucharist worthily or are impeded from so doing. The disposition involved is appropriate for those who follow Mass on television. Actual Communion is clearly not possible in such a circumstance.

Intercommunion

Question: *I was told that Catholics and Orthodox can receive communion in each other's churches. Is this true?*

Answer: Yes and No. The Code of Canon Law (reflecting Roman documents on ecumenism) allows Catholic priests to "administer the sacraments of penance, Eucharist, and anointing of the sick to members of the oriental churches which do not have full communion with the Catholic Church, if they ask on their own for the sacraments and are properly disposed" (Canon 844). Thus an Orthodox Christian may on occasion receive communion in the Catholic Church.

The Code also states: "It is lawful for the [Catholic] faithful for whom it is physically or morally impossible to approach a Catholic minister, to receive the sacraments of penance, Eucharist, and anointing of the sick from non-Catholic ministers in whose churches these sacraments are valid" (Ibid.). Since the Catholic Church recognizes the validity of the Orthodox Eucharist, a Catholic may, in case of necessity, receive Communion in an Orthodox church.

But (with a capital B), the Orthodox churches generally do not allow Catholics (or members of any other denomination) to receive communion in their churches. So for a Catholic to ignore such a prohibition would be to show disrespect for Orthodox regulations. By the same token, Orthodox are generally not allowed by their own leadership to receive communion in a Catholic (or any other) Church.

On the matter of Catholic-Orthodox intercommunion, the U.S. Catholic bishops summed up the matter nicely in their November 1996 Guidelines for the Reception of Communion at a Catholic Mass: "Members of the Orthodox Churches, the Assyrian Church of the East, and the Polish National Catholic Church are urged to respect the discipline of their own Churches. According to Roman Catholic discipline, the Code of Canon Law does not object to the reception of communion by Christians of these Churches."

Communion and Non-Catholics

Question: *I am confused about why the Church does not allow non-Catholics like President Clinton to receive Communion in the Catholic Church. Why were the Irish bishops upset when (Catholic) President Mary McAleese received communion at a Church of Ireland (Anglican) service? Don't confuse me with Canon Law. What's the bottom line here?*

Answer: You want the bottom line? Here it is. The Catholic view of Communion is that in the Eucharist we don't only receive Christ in a personal way. We are also expressing and deepening our commitment to the living Body of Christ, his Church on earth. To receive Communion in the Catholic Church is to affirm publicly all that the Catholic Church believes, teaches, and does. When we walk to the altar of the Lord in a Catholic Church, we are expressing belief in the Catholic doctrine of the real presence of Christ, in Catholic teaching about the authoritative role of the papacy and the episcopacy, in the Catholic moral tradition — in short, in the whole of Catholicism.

Because of this, well-informed and committed non-Catholics would not wish to receive Communion in the

Catholic Church. To do so would be tantamount to a statement that they wish to be Catholics. Similarly, when Irish President McAleese received Communion in the Church of Ireland, she was (if she knew what she was doing) expressing adherence to Anglicanism, including its 49 Articles of Faith which have, shall we say, not very nice things to say about some matters Catholics hold clear, like the Mass.

Now this is a very rough and ready answer. If I had 25 pages to deal with the matter, I would refine the above, dotting the "i's" and crossing the "t's." A lot more needs to be explained. But there's your bottom line.

Ex-Mason at Communion

Question: *My husband was a Mason before we married. He was later baptized. Since he still wears his Masonic ring, he was told by a priest he couldn't go to Communion. Is that true? Now he only ushers. I would like him to go to Communion with me.*

Answer: The Catholic Church and freemasonry have traditionally not been friends. While not true to the same degree in England or America, freemasonry in Europe has had a strongly anti-Christian and anti-clerical disposition. European Freemasons would not be caught dead in a Catholic Church! The 1917 code of Canon Law forbade Catholics from being Masons. This proscription was not carried over to the 1983 Code, probably because in some parts of the world Masonry is more benign and is vague philosophically. While the Congregation for the Doctrine of the Faith referred in 1983 to Masonic membership as a "grave sin," this may not apply in those situations where Masonic groups have a positive attitude to Christianity — as many American Masons do.

If your husband is, as you suggest, no longer a Mason

but simply wears a Masonic ring, and he sees no inconsistency between this practice and his Catholic faith, then he should not stay away from Communion. On the contrary, you should encourage him to go with you.

Communion for the Remarried

Question: *I know people who are divorced and remarried who receive Communion each time they go to Mass. I know this is against the law of the Church. How is it possible to enforce this restriction?*

Answer: Individuals or couples who are divorced and remarried outside the Church should not receive Communion until existing irregularities are sorted out. The best way to "enforce" correct practice is by effective pastoral guidance. Bishops and pastors have a responsibility to educate Catholics in the discipline of the Church. This requires clarity of teaching, an attitude of charity, and an expressed willingness to help people in difficult situations. Divorced and remarried Catholics should never be made to feel as if they do not belong in the Church.

What can a concerned Catholic like yourself do if you are aware of an irregular situation? If you know an individual in the situation you describe fairly well, you could seek a tactful and charitable way to raise the question of the status of the marriage, help him or her understand the irregularities involved, and then encourage an approach to his or her pastor for a "diagnosis" of the situation.

Eucharist for the Divorced

Question: *Can a person receive the Eucharist if he or she was married in the Church for less than one year, then was divorced, and without an annulment was married outside* *the Church a second time for over 40 years? Both spouses are now deceased.*

Answer: Yes, a person in such circumstances may receive the Eucharist. The logic is that no marriage irregularities preventing the reception of Communion in the situation you describe currently exist. Having been away from the sacraments for 40 years, the person in question would appropriately make contact with his or her pastor and receive the Sacrament of Reconciliation.

Now a speech: I have received more questions regarding the situations of people who are divorced and remarried than on any other topic. I quickly determined that it would not be possible to answer most of the questions submitted because of incomplete data.

What is evident, however, is that many people in similar circumstances misunderstand their standing in the Church. Some think they should stay away from the sacraments because of marriage problems when, in fact, there is no impediment to receiving them. (For instance, some Catholics think that the answer to the question above is "no," when in reality it is "yes.") Others think that the very fact of being legally divorced (with no subsequent marriage) prevents them from receiving Communion. It doesn't.

I would encourage anyone whose marriage situation is complicated to approach a wise and kind priest to get a good pastoral "diagnosis" on his or her situation.

Annulments

Question: *Aren't annulments really just "Catholic divorces"? I hear horror stories about how much annulments cost and that only the rich get them. Annulments make children illegitimate! I find all this scandalous.*

Answer: You must have been watching some old Phil Donahue re-runs on this topic! The Catholic Church does not grant divorces (the breaking up of true marriages) but rather annulments (declarations that a valid marriage did not exist). The expression "Catholic divorce" is entirely inappropriate, and the Church is constantly vigilant about abuses creeping into annulment procedures.

It is not true that annulments are expensive and are only given to the rich. A modest fee is generally requested to cover secretarial expenses, but an inability to pay is not an impediment. The poor comprise a large portion of those who seek annulments. Actually, the rich and famous probably have a more difficult time getting annulments because of the dangers of misperception.

In no way does a marriage annulment make children already born illegitimate. Prior to annulment, marriages are considered valid and enjoy positive regard in the Church. Children born of such marriages always retain the benefit of ecclesiastical good standing.

Priests Granting Annulments

Questions: Is it possible for a parish priest to grant an annulment of marriage for someone?

Answer: The answer is "no." The diocesan marriage tribunal is the ordinary agency that may process marriage annulments. Declarations of nullity may be granted by an ecclesiastical tribunal only after a systematic and thorough investigation of all aspects of a marriage. An affirmative decision must be reviewed and approved by a second ecclesiastical court outside the diocese handling the particular annulment.

Situations in which a priest conducts a wedding for anyone in an existing valid marriage represents a serious abuse. If the couple seeking marriage have one or more previous marriages and are in good faith about their upcoming wedding due to the misleading action of the priest, the gravity of the initiative of the latter is compounded.

Pauline Privilege

Questions: Please explain the Pauline Privilege. A friend of mine recently received one. I am very confused about its meaning.

Answer: The Pauline Privilege is an exceptional practice involving the dissolution of the marriage bond of two persons not baptized at the time of their marriage. The basis for the practice is St. Paul's First Letter to the Corinthians (7:12-16), which I encourage you to look up: it's a little long to quote here.

The conditions for the Pauline Privilege are the following: both parties were unbaptized at the time of the marriage; after the marriage one of the parties was baptized, but the other one remained unbaptized; the unbaptized person either abandoned the marriage by divorce or desertion or made married life unbearable for the Christian; the unbaptized person is unwilling to live peacefully with the Christian party.

If the above conditions are fulfilled the Church may grant the baptized person the right to marry another Christian or a non-baptized person.

Renewing Wedding Vows

Question: *I recently attended a Mass with a beautiful renewal of wedding vows in which the couple (married 50 years) said their marriage vows again. My sister (married 49 years) wants the same ceremony next year, but her pastor* *said there is no such ceremony. Please enlighten me on this.*

Answer: I hope your sister's pastor was being kind when he told your sister this, and that he worked out a suitably constructive response to her request!

In fact there exists no such rite as a "renewal of wedding vows" — and for a good reason: wedding vows are not like one's driver's license or passport, which run out every few years and need to be renewed. Wedding vows are forever. Rites of renewal of wedding vows are, in my opinion, apt to be misleading in a culture of divorce and remarriage.

The Church does provide, however, an official Order for the Blessing of a Married Couple on the anniversary of marriage. In this blessing, vows are not formally repeated, and I think it unwise to insert such vows into the rite. Rings may be exchanged in this ceremony (rings, unlike vows, do wear out). This rite has the character of thanksgiving for what God has done in the life of the couple and intercession for the years ahead.

"Best Nun" at Wedding

Question: *At a Catholic church wedding recently the best man was a nun. She was called "the Best Nun." The bridesmaid was a woman. Is this allowed? What do you think of this practice?*

Answer: Let us consult two authorities here.

Authority Number 1: *The Code of Canon Law.* The various relevant canons of the Code require two witnesses for marriage; these must be physically present; they must have the use of reason and be capable of understanding what is going on.

There is nothing that requires that both sexes be represented as witnesses. A religious sister is not prevented from acting as a witness to a marriage. So, as far as witnesses are concerned, there was nothing irregular about the wedding you describe.

Authority Number 2: *Miss Primm's Handbook for Excruciatingly Correct Weddings.* Miss Primm thinks it exceedingly inappropriate to flout the custom of having a male best man and a female matron/maid of honor. She believes resolutely in tradition and considers doing ostentatiously "untraditional" things at weddings to be frivolous, disrespectful of such a weighty occasion, and probably indicative of a need for attention on the part of one or more persons in the wedding party.

Miss Primm thinks the notion of a matrimonial "Best Nun" should have the same level of social acceptance as women wrestlers. Miss Primm would allow for exceptions to the rule in unusual and unpredictable circumstances (e.g., a wedding on the Titanic after the band has stopped playing, or between aftershocks following an earthquake).

What do I think? I'm staying neutral. But I'd like to know if a guy has ever acted as a bridesmaid (or bridesperson). If anyone has seen this, send a photograph.

Minor Orders?

Question: *What are minor orders? Do they still exist? Do parish lectors have these orders?*

Answer: Traditionally, the minor orders were preparatory stages for candidates for the priesthood. They included porter, reader, exorcist, and acolyte and were conferred on priesthood candidates by a bishop at various intervals in the first years of seminary formation.

The minor orders (first mentioned in the writings of Pope Cornelius in the third century) came into existence as official recognition of specific offices in the church. The minor orders were abolished in 1972. They were replaced by the ministries of acolyte and lector, which are now formally conferred on candidates for the priesthood.

In the U.S. these roles have not to my knowledge been officially conferred on (any of the thousands of) non-priesthood candidates who actually carry on the roles of lector and acolyte in parishes — which in no way takes away from the baptismal dignity or integrity of these lay roles.

Divorced Priestly Candidates

Question: *Can a divorced man become a priest? I heard that the bishop in our diocese was going to allow it.*

Answer: Only in very exceptional circumstances could a divorced man become a priest. Canon 1041 of the Code of Canon Laws includes the following as irregular for the reception of holy orders: "a person who has attempted marriage, even a civil one only, either while he was impeded from entering marriage due to an existing matrimonial bond, sacred orders or a public perpetual vow of chastity, or with a woman bound by a valid marriage or by the same type of vow."

Put simply: a Catholic cannot walk out on wife and children (whether he was married in the Catholic Church or in Las Vegas), get a divorce, study for the priesthood, and be ordained.

The very particular circumstance in which the scenario you describe could occur would be the following: a man has been married; he is now divorced; he has received an ecclesiastical annulment from his marriage; and he has discharged all his obligations (spiritual and material) to his "ex-wife" and/or children.

However, if the reasons for the marriage annulment were rooted in the man's own psychological immaturity or instability, this would disqualify him from being a candidate for ordination.

Laicization of Clergy

Question: *A priest in Dallas was recently laicized. I thought this practice was abolished. Isn't the term insulting to us "laity"?*

Answer: The act of "reducing" a member of the clergy to "lay" status has not been abolished. In extraordinary circumstances and to serve the general good of the church, the Holy See may laicize a bishop, priest, or deacon. The laicized person does not, however, lose his sacramental powers and maintains ordained status.

He is, however, dispensed from the ordinary duties of his office, and generally also from celibacy, allowing him to marry. In an emergency situation, a laicized priest may validly administer the sacraments of reconciliation and the anointing of the sick.

I can understand how the term "laicization" — along with the language of "reduction" to the lay state — can appear insulting to the "laity." Better terms might be devised. The more colorful term "defrock" was often used popularly in the past, but it lacks, should we say, a certain gravity. Your point is a valid one.

Sacraments of the Dead

Question: *Why are some sacraments called "sacraments of the dead"? I thought you had to be alive to receive the sacraments. How does this relate to Mormon baptism for the dead?*

Answer: The term "sacraments of the dead" traditionally refers to sacraments which may be received when a person is not in the state of grace. These include baptism, reconciliation, and the anointing of the sick. These sacraments serve among other things to overcome whatever alienation from God may exist in a person's life.

The term "sacraments of the living" refer to sacraments that require the recipient to be in a state of grace before properly receiving them: Confirmation, the Eucharist, matrimony, and holy orders.

The Mormon practice of "baptism for the dead" has nothing to do with the Catholic notion of "sacraments of the dead." For Catholics the latter term refers to spiritual, not physical death. Those who have physically died have passed beyond the realm of sacraments into the providence of God.

The traditional division between sacraments of the "living" and of the "dead" is not, in my opinion, particularly useful and can be misleading — as your own question implies. There are more adequate ways of making the essential point.

Lay Last Rites?

Question: *When no priest is available to administer the last rites to a dying person, what should one do?*

Question: *Is it permissible for a eucharistic minister to administer the Last Rites to an accident victim if a priest cannot get there?*

Answer: If by "Last Rites," you mean the sacrament of Anointing of the Sick, the answer is "no." The sacramental rite of Anointing of the Sick always requires a priest or deacon.

If, on the other hand, you mean the prayers used when someone is dying — which is what the Church officially means by Last Rites — the answer is that all lay Catholics (not just eucharistic ministers) can perform these rites.

When a priest or deacon is not present, one should do what Catholics have always done: say the prayers oneself. I am constantly amazed and edified at the ability of Hispanic Catholics (as well as Catholics from more traditional cultures) to do this, whereas "mainstream" American Catholics often stand helplessly by and don't know what to do.

I strongly recommend that every Catholic household obtain a copy of the little book entitled *Pastoral Care of the Sick: Rites of Anointing and Viaticum* (available through your local Catholic bookstore). Chapter 6 contains prayers for the "Commendation of the Dying." These prayers are very powerful and among the most moving in all of the Church's rites.

The Introduction to the book states that if a priest or deacon is unavailable, "other members of the community should be prepared to assist with these prayers and should have the texts readily available to them" (no. 213).

Every Catholic would do well to become familiar with these prayers for emergency situations. You might suggest to your pastor or religious education director that the parish put on an evening workshop on this matter for parishioners.

FIVE

Liturgy

General
Art and Environment
Liturgical Year
Mass
Funerals

Liturgical Movement

Question: *I read that the liturgical movement before Vatican II was agitating for changes in the Mass. Is this where all the troubles we have now began?*

Answer: You and I would need to discuss what you think are the current "troubles" in the liturgy before I could answer your question with complete adequacy. However, if you are a subscriber to *Our Sunday Visitor* I assume you are a moderate and reasonable person.

The liturgical movement has its roots in the work of the nineteenth century French Benedictine Abbot Prosper Guéranger to bring about a spiritual renewal of liturgical life in an era in which the liturgical discipline of the Church was not in great shape (to put it mildly). This cause was taken up by Pope Pius X in the early twentieth century when he revived Gregorian chant and encouraged frequent Communion.

A whole host of outstanding scholars carried the liturgical movement through the first half of the twentieth century, seeking to uncover the liturgical traditions of early Christianity, developing familiarity with the rich traditions of the East, and examining the biblical and theological roots of the liturgy. Figures like Pius Parsch in Austria and Virgil Michel in the U.S. ensured that these concerns were always connected to actual parish renewal.

The Constitution on the Sacred Liturgy of Vatican II was the fruit of the accumulated results of the liturgical movement of the previous century. The changes for which the liturgical movement was "agitating" (not a word I would choose) found their way into the Vatican II Constitution.

Some who dislike the modern liturgy blame Vatican II and the liturgical movement for the current "troubles." As a strong admirer of the liturgical movement, I do not share this assessment. What is troublesome in the church's liturgical life today derives primarily, in my view, from a certain cultural corruption of the liturgy. Indeed, were the Church to renew its connections to the preconciliar liturgical movement, Catholic worship would, I propose, be greatly enriched.

Handling Liturgical Abuses

Question: *I find myself being constantly annoyed and irritated by liturgical abuses in my parish. Please help me to handle this. Should I write to the bishop?*

Answer: Liturgical abuses (whether in the form of unauthorized adaptations or general sloppiness) understandably cause annoyance and irritation.

What can one do? First, remind oneself that the liturgy is the action of Christ and that Christ is present and active even in the midst of most of the common abuses. Second, pray for those (whether clergy or laity) who fail to respect the integrity of the liturgy. Apart from its efficacious power, prayer takes anger and hostility out of the heart and makes life more bearable. Third, find a way to express one's concerns to those involved in a reasonable, well-informed, and charitable manner. This might not (unfortunately) always be very effective, but it beats ranting and raving.

Should one ever complain to the bishop? Yes, when all else fails. Bishops take seriously their responsibility for the liturgical life of parishes, and they are usually sensitive to communications that are reasonable, prudent, and brief. However, no bishop has time or energy for a ten-page diatribe.

Ad-libbing at Mass

Question: *When may a priest "ad-lib" during Mass? Are*

there rules? Our priest never stops ad-libbing things all through Mass.

Answer: The problem you mention is a serious and pervasive one. We live in an entertainment-oriented, talk-show culture, so it's not surprising that priests should be affected by this. The Church seeks to protect both the liturgy and the people from priestly "ad-libbing" by carefully limiting the opportunity for "creative" improvisation.

The General Instruction of the Roman Missal authorizes the priest to offer the following introduction in his own words: first, he may very briefly introduce the Mass of the day (before the celebration begins); second, he may introduce the liturgy of the word (before the readings); third, he may introduce the eucharistic prayer (before the preface); and, fourth, he may make concluding remarks before the dismissal (no. 11).

Regarding other admonitions, the Appendix to the General Instruction for the Dioceses of the United States state: "The Order of Mass provides others as well, which are important to certain portions of the rite, such as during the penitential rite, or before the Lord's Prayer. By their very nature these brief admonitions do not require that everyone use them in the form in which they appear in the Missal. Provision can be made in certain cases that they be adapted to some degree to the varying circumstances of the community. In all cases it is well to remember the nature of an admonition, and not make them into a sermon or homily; care should be taken to keep them brief and not too wordy, for otherwise they become tedious" (no. 11).

A priest who "ad-libs" all the way through Mass is not respecting the relatively restrictive norms provided by official liturgical legislation.

Priestly Holiness

Question: *If the priest is a sinner or not a very holy man, does that affect the Mass?*

Answer: If the efficacy of the Mass depended on the holiness or goodness of priests, the Church would be in deep trouble. The Council of Trent declared (thankfully) that "The sacrament is not wrought by the righteousness of either the celebrant or the recipient, but by the power of God."

The *Catechism of the Catholic Church* spells this out: "From the moment that a sacrament is celebrated in accordance with the intention of the Church, the power of Christ and his Spirit acts in and through it, independently of the personal holiness of the minister" (no. 1128).

The *Catechism* explains further: "Celebrated worthily in faith, the sacraments confer the grace that they signify. They are *efficacious* because in them Christ himself is at work: it is he who baptizes, he who acts in his sacraments in order to communicate the grace that each sacrament signifies" (no. 1127).

Certainly a lack of priestly holiness (especially if it is pervasive or publicly evident) is hardly conducive to the spiritual edification of the people. In this respect, the pastoral effect of the Mass may be somewhat compromised. Nevertheless, the fundamental and objective efficacy of the Mass as an act of Christ remains unaffected by the holiness of the priest, or lack thereof.

Pink Vestments

Question: *In the old days, priests used to wear pink chasubles on some Sundays. Where did the tradition come from? Is it still allowed today? Our young priest bought a very ornate pink chasuble.*

Answer: First, priests wore not pink but rose-colored chasubles. (Pink is not a guy color, excepting people like Brett "The Hit Man" Hart of professional wrestling fame.)

Rose was traditionally worn on "Gaudete Sunday," the third Sunday of Advent, so named from the opening word of the Introit "*Gaudete*" ("Rejoice"). The rose color was also worn on the fourth Sunday of Lent, "Laetare Sunday", the first word of the introductory antiphon being "*Laetare*" ("Rejoice").

The general purpose of these days was to provide a respite from the rigors of Advent and Lent. Rose vestments may still be used on those days, but most priests choose to stay with the seasonal color (violet). When it comes to priestly vestments, my own tastes are fairly "low church": simple materials, plain colors, minimal decoration.

I hope your young priest put as much work into his homilies and the other aspects of his liturgical and pastoral ministry as he does into his liturgical wardrobe.

Tabernacle's Place

Question: *According to the* Catechism of the Catholic Church, *the Eucharist is the "source and summit" of the Christian life. If this is so, why is it that, in some Catholic churches, the tabernacle is not the focal point, but is either off on a side altar, or not in the main church at all?*

Answer: The *Catechism* quote to which you refer focuses not primarily on the place of the tabernacle but on the truth that liturgy is not all there is to Christian life.

It states: "The sacred liturgy does not exhaust the entire activity of the Church: it must be preceded by evangelization, faith, and conversion. It can then produce its fruits in the lives of the faithful: new life in the Spirit, involvement in the mission of the Church, and service to her unity" (no. 1072).

However, your question about the place of the tabernacle is appropriate. The fundamental issue is the right balance between altar and tabernacle in a Catholic Church.

If the tabernacle tended to dominate the altar before Vatican II, it is not surprising (given the tendency of pendulums to swing) that since the council the tabernacle has often been underemphasized.

Off-Center Altar

Question: *Does it not demean the Blessed Sacrament and the Mass when the main altar is off-center and replaced by flowers and a water fountain?*

Answer: Not necessarily. A variety of floor plans have existed in Catholic churches over the centuries, and we should not expect that the evolution of church architecture has ended.

There is nothing to prevent an altar being off-center as long as it is dignified in style and prominent in location. Nor is there anything to prevent a baptismal font in a central place in the sanctuary.

A lot depends on why this arrangement was devised and how it is being understood in the parish. If the point is to highlight the dignity of baptism, that's fair enough. If the point is to say that the Eucharist is secondary to baptism, then there is a problem. Sometimes such arrangements want to point out the complementarity of the word and the sacrament by balancing ambo and altar — a harmless, if not particularly earth-shattering, principle.

As a practical matter, off-center altars do not function very well. They can be difficult to see, and their non-symmetrical appearance gets old fast.

No Pews?

Question: *After attending Mass in cathedrals and basilicas in numerous European countries where there weren't any pews, my question is this: When and where were pews introduced into Catholic churches?*

Answer: From the beginning of Christian worship, some form or other of seating was provided for particular people. In the earliest period, benches for the aged and infirm were often placed along the wall. While chairs were used by the bishop and other ministers, seats were seldom available for the whole community. After the fourth century, seating was provided for the emperor and other dignitaries. In the following centuries, benches were installed for monks or clerics who occupied the choir area in front of the altar. Evidence exists that after the ninth century scattered benches or stools were provided for the laity, mostly the upper classes. During the fourteenth and fifteenth centuries, the use of fixed seats became more widespread. Churches filled with pews and kneelers became common after the sixteenth century, generally more in Protestant than in Catholic churches.

Kneeling

Question: *In our parish we were taught that kneeling is not a Christian practice, but that it started with slaves forced to kneel to their masters in pagan Egypt. What is the meaning of kneeling?*

Answer: Kneeling is a natural symbol of the veneration of the greatness of God and a basic posture of prayer. In harmony with fairly universal human feeling and numerous Old and New Testament references, kneeling has been practiced in Christian worship from the beginning as an expression of penitence and supplication. The history of kneeling in Christian worship is quite complicated, but it has remained a fundamental liturgical and devotional posture for 2,000 years.

I doubt that anyone has reliable documentation that kneeling was invented in ancient Egypt. And if they had, so what? I assume pagans ate dinner, occasionally washed themselves, and kept the cat off the kitchen table. Does that make these intrinsically pagan practices reprehensible to Christians? Hardly! If Christians have knelt in prayer for two millennia, the practice may reasonably be called Christian.

Crosses in Churches

Question: *Our parish church is being renovated. The liturgical consultant says that the only cross in the church has to be a processional cross and that there can be no permanent crucifix on the wall. Is this correct?*

Answer: Your author (who is also a liturgical consultant) responds: No, it's not. The General Instruction of the Roman Missal assumes that the principal cross for liturgical use will be a processional cross (nos. 84, 270). The U.S. Bishops' Committee on the Liturgy document "Environment and Art in Catholic Worship" assumes the same (no. 88).

However, that a permanent cross, that is, one that is non-processional, may also be placed in a church is consistent with the following statement of the General Instruction: "In accord with ancient tradition, images of Christ, Mary, and the saints are venerated in churches" (no. 278). In tandem with this, one may refer to the Ceremonial of Bishops, which contains the following statement: "Of all sacred images, the 'figure of the precious, life-giving cross of Christ' is preeminent, because it is the symbol of the entire paschal mystery. The cross is the image most cherished by the Christian people and the most ancient; it represents Christ's suffering and victory, and at the same time, as the Fathers of the Church have taught, it points to his Second Coming" (no. 1011).

Should such a cross be a crucifix? The answer is yes, as a rule. The official Book of Blessings states: "The image of the cross should preferably be a crucifix, that is, have the corpus attached, especially in the case of a cross that is erected in a place of honor inside a church" (no. 1235).

Recorded Music in Church

Question: *Is the use of recorded music allowed in the liturgy? This is happening a lot in my parish. The pastor just installed a big CD player.*

Answer: There is very little in the official documents of the Church on the topic of the liturgical use of recorded music for the simple reason that this kind of practice was until recently inconceivable.

Let me quote from the 1995 Snowbird Statement on Catholic Liturgical Music written by seventeen musicians and liturgists from various parts of the English-speaking world. This is an excellent document (but your author would think that, since he was one of its editors!). On the matter you raise, it states: "The use of recorded music is a great temptation in Catholic worship today, especially where adequate musical resources are lacking. This option, attractive as it may appear, should be discouraged as antithetical to the nature of the liturgy as the living act of God's people. Nothing should substitute for or impede the functioning of the assembly in actual liturgical celebrations. The use of recorded choirs, organs and cantors, though they can seem to serve an immediate need, has the effect of discouraging local communities from marshalling the resources necessary for the authentic celebration of the liturgy."

Recorded music in worship, canned homilies, plastic flowers, and electric candles all belong in the same category: Bad Liturgical Practices.

Sacred and Profane

Question: *Please help me understand the difference between the sacred and the profane. Are concerts in churches profane?*

Answer: The sacred is that which positively pertains to God; the profane is that which is distorted in its relationship to God.

Christianity (unlike some religions) does not make an absolute distinction between sacred and profane. It looks instead to human intentions and motivations.

The Judeo-Christian vision is of creation as holy, since God is the author of all things. Profane literally means "outside the temple." But for Christians all creation is, in an important respect, the temple of God.

Human beings, however, can distort the potential goodness of things. Accordingly, the holiness or profanity of created realities is not so much in the things themselves. In great part, it is what human beings do with them that makes them sacred or profane.

Consider, for instance, the ordinary reality of water. Water as a created entity is in itself neutral. Blessed for baptism, water becomes holy; but used to drown your grandmother, it is profane.

A concert in the church by a group that has made a name for itself for excess on MTV would most likely be profane for the reason that the lyrics and general musical chaos would be difficult to reconcile with the dignity of the church and the worship of God. A performance in a church of music by great classical masters would not be profane if the compositions were in sympathy with noble ideals and conception of life (even if not explicitly religious).

Missals at Mass

Question: *My pastor says we should not be reading from missals at Mass but should simply listen to the readings and prayers. What does the Church teach about this?*

Answer: Nothing. In *Sacrosanctum Concilium* (Constitution on the Sacred Liturgy), Vatican II called Catholics to "full, conscious and active participation in liturgical celebrations" (no. 14).

There are many ways to achieve this goal. While it is not desirable to spend the entire Mass with one's nose stuck in a book, it seems unwise of pastors and liturgists to outlaw the use of missals.

There are many situations in which missals are useful: if one has a hearing impediment, if the sound system in the church is inadequate, or if the readers or clergy speak indistinctly.

If missals genuinely aid fuller appreciation of the liturgical texts and assist the active participation of worshipers, then their use is, in my opinion, quite acceptable.

Evening Masses

Question: *Where did evening Masses come from? Don't Saturday and Sunday evening Masses destroy the idea of the Lord's Day?*

Answer: Because the Mass had its origin in the Last Supper, it was natural for the early church to retain the evening hour for the celebration of the Eucharist. Until the Middle Ages,

Mass was celebrated in the late afternoon on the weekdays of Lent. Not until the turn of the fifteenth century did evening Mass disappear. In 1566 it was finally prohibited by Pope Pius V. The prohibition was codified in the old 1917 Code of Canon Law (Canon 821).

However a variety of circumstances, such as persecution of the church in Mexico in 1927 and in Russia in 1929 and World War II, modified the prohibition. The modern pattern of life and work, unlike that of earlier times, makes the morning a less suitable time for Mass for everybody. Gradually it became necessary to give more extensive permission for evening Masses. In 1957 this permission became general for all days of the week.

Evening Masses on Saturdays and Sundays ought to be considered exceptional practices for the very reason you mention. Unfortunately, the exception has become the norm in many people's thinking and practice. In my opinion, the increasing loss of the integrity of Sunday as the Lord's Day is a serious problem.

Televised Mass

Question: *Being 82 years old, may I "attend" the TV Mass at home in place of going to church? Do we honor the Blessed Sacrament on TV the same way as we do in church, even if the Mass was taped?*

Answer: Last year, the U.S. bishops issued a document on exactly this topic with the title "Guidelines for Televising the Liturgy." The bishops state: "Televising the Mass is a ministry by which the Church uses modern technology to bring the Lord's healing and comfort to those who cannot physically participate in the liturgical life of the local church."

If you are unable to attend Mass without hardship, then participating in the Mass by television is commendable. The more reverently and prayerfully you can participate the better. You might even light a candle in your living room while the Mass is going on. (But be careful not to burn the house down!)

The bishops encourage Mass to be televised "live." In this way, "the viewer is able to join in the prayer of a worshiping community as the liturgy is celebrated." However, one should be no less reverent and prayerful in watching a taped Mass, and one's veneration of the Blessed Sacrament should be just as real.

It is most important that your pastor be aware of your inability to attend Mass, so that arrangements can be made to have Communion brought to you on a regular basis. The bishops state: "The televised Mass is never a substitute for the Church's pastoral care for the sick in the form of visits by parish ministers who share the Scriptures and bring Communion."

Attending Non-Catholic Worship

Question: *My daughter's education places her in an area where there is no Catholic Church available. On those occasions, would it be wrong for her to attend a non-Catholic church service?*

Answer: I would recommend, first, that your daughter call the local Catholic diocese and explain the problem. It may be that Mass is celebrated somewhere in her vicinity without her knowing it. Her call might also inform the diocese of a need of which it might not be aware.

If an Eastern Catholic church (in communion with Rome) or an Eastern Orthodox church (not in communion with Rome, but having valid sacraments) exists in the area, this would be an appropriate option (However, Orthodox churches generally prohibit non-Orthodox from receiving Communion).

Attending a Protestant church on occasion is not totally out of the question. However, communion should never be received. Gathering together with other Catholics for morning prayer or for a Sunday service in the absence of a priest (with the diocese's approval) are the solutions I would recommend.

Ordinary Time
Question: *Why are most Sundays of the year called "Ordinary" Sundays? Surely Sunday should be special and extraordinary.*

Answer: The Sundays of Advent/Christmas and Lent/Easter celebrate particular aspects or dimensions of the mysteries of faith. The other Sundays of the year do not. They celebrate rather the whole mystery of faith. These are called Ordinary, not in the sense of being unimportant or less significant, but in the sense of being normative or standard (by comparison to which the Advent/Christmas and Lent/Easter Sundays are extraordinary).

The Constitution on the Sacred Liturgy of Vatican II spoke of Sunday as "the original feast day" and "the foundation and kernel of the whole liturgical year" (no. 106). Ordinary Sundays are properly regarded as the norm on which everything else in the liturgical year is built. Ordinary Time may be taken to mean Standard Liturgical Time.

Holy Day Confusion
Question: *I am confused about the number of holy days. Some have obligations one year but not the next. Why are some holy days on Sundays?*

Answer: The 1983 Code of Canon Law lists ten holy days of obligation for the universal church: "The Nativity of Our Lord Jesus Christ, the Epiphany, the Ascension and the Most Holy Body and Blood of Christ, Holy Mary Mother of God and her Immaculate Conception and Assumption, Saint Joseph, the Apostles Saints Peter and Paul, and finally, all Saints" (Canon 1246). However, the Code goes on to say, "The conference of bishops can abolish certain holy days of obligation or transfer them to a Sunday with prior approval of the Apostolic See" (ibid.).

By "abolish" here is meant that the conference of bishops can abrogate the obligation attached to one of the feasts listed, but not the feast itself. When certain holy days occur on Saturdays or Mondays, the obligation for that year may be suspended in order to avoid imposing undue hardship on people. The bishops' conference may (following certain norms) transfer some holy days to Sundays in order to encourage greater popular participation.

In the U.S., there are six holy days of obligation: Christmas (December 25); Mary, Mother of God (January 1); Ascension (Thursday in the Sixth Week of Easter —except, since 1995, in the western United States, where it occurs on the Seventh Sunday of Easter); Assumption (August 15); All Saints (November 1), and Immaculate Conception (December 8).

Buildings or People?

Question: *Recently when we celebrated the Feast of the Dedication of the Basilica of St. John Lateran, the homilist said it was "foolish" to celebrate buildings and not people. What is your response to that?*

Answer: The Church never celebrates buildings apart from the people who worship in them. The prayers, readings, and blessings used in the dedication of churches and church furnishings make the strong and unmistakable point that liturgical buildings exist to build up the people of God, themselves the living temples of the Holy Spirit. This thinking is firmly rooted in the New Testament epistles (see 1 Cor 3:9-17; Eph 2:19-22; Heb 12:18-24; 1 Pt 2:4-9).

The church building is, we might say, a model of the Christian soul. Caesarius of Arles, writing in the sixth century, made this point very graphically: "Whenever we come to church, we must prepare our hearts to be as beautiful as we expect this church to be. Do you wish to find this basilica immaculately clean? Then do not soil your soul with the filth of sins. Do you wish this basilica to be full of light? God too wishes that your soul be not in darkness, but that the light of good works shine in us, so that he who dwells in the heavens will be glorified. Just as you enter this church building, so God wishes to enter into your soul, for he promised: I shall live in them, and I shall walk the corridors of their heart" (Sermon 229). This passage appears in the Office of Readings for — guess what day? — the Feast of the Dedication of Saint John Lateran.

Holy Week Obligation?

Question: *If Holy Thursday, Good Friday, and Holy Saturday are not holy days of obligation, does this not lessen their importance for Catholics?*

Answer: Not unless one believes that legality is everything. Those days are not days of obligation for the following reasons: obligations are not attached to liturgies other than the Mass (Mass is never celebrated on Good Friday); while the Easter Vigil is part of Easter Sunday, there is no obligation to participate in any particular Easter Mass; the Holy

Thursday Mass of the Lord's Supper is the only Mass celebrated on that day, thus an obligation to attend that Mass would be unrealistic.

In recent decades, and certainly since the Second Vatican Council (1962-65) the high emphasis given to the latter days of Holy Week should generate in Catholics an internal sense of obligation to participate as fully as possible in the Triduum liturgies. The General Norms for the Liturgical Year and the Calendar state that the Easter Triduum of the passion and resurrection of Christ is "the culmination of the entire liturgical year. What Sunday is to the week, the Solemnity of Easter is to the liturgical year" (no. 18).

Women and Foot Washing

Question: *I was under the impression that at the Holy Thursday washing of feet, only men should be included. At our parish, both men and women have their feet washed. Please clarify.*

Answer: The instruction in the Sacramentary for Holy Thursday states: "The men who have been chosen are led by the ministers to chairs prepared in a suitable place. Then the priest . . . goes to each man. With the help of the ministers, he pours water over each one's feet and dries them."

Whether what is envisaged here is the washing of the feet of males only or of "men" generically (which includes women) has been a matter of debate.

Since definitive rulings have not been issued by the Vatican Congregation for Worship and the Discipline of the Sacraments, the matter remains open.

My own opinion is that there exist no theological grounds that would exclude the washing of women's feet. The liturgy of Holy Thursday is not a Passion play requiring that the apostles be represented by men, but a celebration of Christ's ongoing service to the whole Church, which includes men and women.

Sister Presiding

Question: *On Good Friday our pastoral associate, a religious sister, was the celebrant and homilist at the evening service. Our pastor sat in the front pew and only moved to help her carry the cross for veneration. She sat in the priest's chair. Is this something new, and is it liturgically correct?*

Answer: This is indeed something new, and no, it is not liturgically correct. Your account suggests that this was not Stations of the Cross (which a non-ordained person could lead), but the actual Celebration of the Lord's Passion. Only in the absence of a priest or deacon may a religious sister, brother, or lay person conduct an official liturgy of the church.

In a situation in which no priest or deacon is able to be present for the official Good Friday liturgy, the bishop may authorize someone else to lead and preach. However, no church leader faithful to ecclesiastical norms would authorize the kind of arrangement you describe.

A non-ordained person leading the liturgy with the pastor in the congregation creates confusion about leadership roles in the church and suggests that the agenda of advancing women's roles in the church might have been (inappropriately) operative in the particular circumstances.

Paschal Candle

Question: *I noticed that there is a lot of symbolism on the Easter candle in our church. What does it mean? Are plastic Easter candles allowed?*

Answer: The large paschal candle, symbolic of the risen Christ, is blessed and lit at the beginning of each Easter Vigil and placed in a special place near the altar until Pentecost. The candle is ornamented with five large grains of incense, representing the five wounds of Christ, inserted in the form of a cross. The Greek letters Alpha and Omega, symbolizing Christ as the "beginning" and "end" of all things are placed at the top and bottom of the design of the cross. The current year is indicated in the quadrants formed by the cross to signify that Christ's death and resurrection are alive in power today, as they always will be until the end of time.

I've never heard of plastic Easter candles, but I've heard of metal ones (you just pop in a new candle upheld by a spring each year and probably stick on a new date). Such candles belong in the category of "The Tacky." Call me old-fashioned or uppity, but I and the Church recommend the real thing.

Sequences at Mass

Question: *I have noticed that on some Sundays of the year there is something called the "Sequence." Mainly I hear it on Easter and Pentecost Sundays. Can you explain what it is, and why it is only on these two Sundays?*

Answer: Sequences are in origin hymns appended to the Alleluia of the Mass. These first developed as words added to complex Alleluia melodies. The "*Victimae Paschali*" of Easter Sunday and the "*Veni Sancte Spiritus*" of Pentecost are the only remaining examples of obligatory sequences today. These occur after the second reading and before the Alleluia or Gospel Acclamation. Both of these texts are very beautiful and the words are sometimes printed in hymnals and worship aids. Optional sequences in the present liturgy are provided for Corpus Christi (*"Lauda Sion"*) and Our Lady of Sorrows (*"Stabat Mater"*).

Sequences became very popular during the tenth century, so that by the later Middle Ages, there was one for almost every Sunday. Most of these did not survive the reform of the liturgy of Pius V, who issued the so-called Tridentine Missal in 1570. The *"Dies Irae"* was one of the more famous that did survive up to the reforms that followed Vatican II, but is no longer used.

Ascension Sunday

Question: *Last year, I was visiting Boise and tried to go to Mass on Ascension Thursday, only to find that there was no Mass. Ascension Thursday was transferred to Sunday. Can you explain the origin of this practice and what you think of it? Being from near Boston, where we still have Ascension Thursday, I was confused.*

Answer: Being confused is certainly not a condition peculiar to Bostonians. On the matter at hand, the confusion is understandable. In December 1993, Rome granted an indult to the dioceses of the ecclesiastical provinces of Los Angeles, San Francisco, Portland in Oregon, Seattle, and Anchorage to transfer the Ascension to the seventh Sunday of Easter. The provision was made on an experimental basis for a period of five years. The general motivation was to increase public participation in the celebration of the Ascension.

In 1998, the United States Conference of Catholic Bishops approved a procedure (confirmed by Rome) to allow each ecclesiastical province to determine whether or not to make the change permanent. By a count made in 2000, most provinces had made the change. The exceptions were the provinces of Boston, Hartford, New York, Newark,

Philadelphia, Baltimore, Washington, D.C., Atlanta, and Omaha, which retained the traditional arrangement.

What do I think? I did not then nor do I now support the move of Ascension Day to Sunday for a number of reasons. First, the move upsets a long and venerable tradition, thus destabilizing the liturgical calendar. Second, the change tampers with the symbolism of the "Forty Days" (Why not then abolish all numerical symbolism in the liturgy?).

Third, the danger of Catholicism becoming a "Sunday Religion" is increased. The calendar of faith should overflow into our ordinary weekday calendars. Fourth, the notion that more people will participate in Ascension doesn't stand up to scrutiny for the reason that those who believe in observing Ascension would have continued to observe it on a weekday, while those who don't are not particularly interested when they encounter it on the seventh Sunday of Easter.

However, being the docile son of the Church that I am, I am going along with the change, and will make the best of it.

Talking Before Mass

Question: *In our parish, talking in church before Mass is encouraged. The pastor and "greeters" go up and down the aisles asking people to introduce themselves. Is this allowed? Where did this practice come from?*

Answer: How common this practice is in Catholic churches in the U.S. and how it began, I am uncertain. Commendable motives generally undergird such activity: getting people to know each other, breaking down distance between pastors and people, ensuring that churches are hospitable and welcoming environments. These aims deserve to be worked on assiduously in every parish.

Is the period just before Mass in church appropriate for

such activity? I don't think so. The Church's liturgical norms are, however, silent on this matter. They appear simply to assume the long-standing tradition of worshipers reverently entering the church and quietly preparing themselves for Mass. This tradition is, in my opinion, most worthy of continuance and promotion.

The time before Mass is not "empty time" (as before a concert or a basketball game), but a period in which the worshiper prepares his or her soul for the great mystery to be celebrated.

Besides, not everyone likes the practice you describe. Some people are embarrassed, annoyed, or feel overly exposed by it. People have been known to avoid churches in which excessive greeting goes on before and during Mass. The liturgy has to be respectful of all personality types: not just the gregarious and outgoing, but the shy, timid, and reserved.

Priest or Presider?

Question: *Our pastor recently informed us in a homily that the people are the celebrants of the Mass — not the priest. He said the proper word for the priest is the "presider." Is this correct?*

Answer: The word "celebrant" was used typically before the Second Vatican Council (1962-65) to refer to the role of the priest at the altar.

Since the council (largely through a recovery of early Christian thought), it has become customary to speak of the whole people of God gathered in worship as "celebrants" of the liturgy.

Which view is correct? Both are. Your pastor is correct in stating that the people are celebrants at Mass, but wrong in saying that he himself should not be spoken of as "celebrant."

It would be equally unsound to say that the priest is

celebrant in any sense exclusive of the people. Priest and people are celebrants in clearly distinct manners: one by ordination, the others by baptism.

Read nos. 1136-1144 of the *Catechism* on this matter. There we are told that Christ, the eternal high priest, as well as the angels and saints, the whole Church on earth, the local congregation, and the priest all celebrate the liturgy in a harmonious yet hierarchically ordered manner.

The priest may indeed be spoken of as "presider," the only authentic meaning of which is that he is priest-celebrant.

Concelebrants

Question: *There are lots of visiting concelebrating priests at our parish, and the pastor likes to introduce them at the beginning of Mass. I find this irritating. Am I wrong?*

Answer: In my opinion, your irritation is not unfounded. Worshipers are naturally curious about visiting clergy. Their curiosity can be alleviated at the announcement time at the end of Mass — which, I suggest, is the point at which concelebrants or any other visitors are appropriately introduced.

As I see it, there are two arguments against introducing concelebrants at the beginning of Mass. First, it distracts from attention on Father, Son, and Holy Spirit, who should be our primary concern.

At a Mass I recently concelebrated, the greeting in the name of the Trinity was rushed through while I was given a round of applause. I was appreciative, but, like Queen Victoria, "not amused."

Second, the practice of priestly introductions is somewhat clericalist. Why only introduce clergy and not all visitors? Of course, some parishes do exactly that (which is a whole other problem).

In brief, at the beginning of Mass, priests and people should keep their focus on the worship of God, and chatter should be kept to a minimum.

The Meaning of Incense

Question: *In our new parish, the priest uses incense every Sunday. Why is incense used? Where does the practice come from? What does it mean? When can it be used?*

Answer: The fragrant cloud of smoke produced in Christian worship symbolizes prayer rising to God. Psalm 141 has the words, "Let my prayer be counted as incense before thee." We read in the Book of Revelation: "and the smoke of the incense rose with the prayers of the saints from the hands of the angel before God" (8:4). Abundant references to incense exist in the Old Testament.

Incense may be used at any Mass, though it is rarely used on weekdays. Its use is prescribed for the rite of commendation and farewell which concludes a funeral Mass. Whenever exposition with Benediction of the Blessed Sacrament takes place, incense is used.

Kissing the Altar

Question: *Why does the priest kiss the altar at the beginning of Mass? Where does the practice come from? Someone said it's a sign that the priest is married to the Church and that the altar stands for the priest's bride.*

Answer: In the ancient world the kiss as a form of greeting was used to show reverence for temples and images of the gods. Its transference to the Christian altar can be traced to the fourth century. In the Middle Ages, the practice was encouraged by the fact that the altar was looked upon as a symbol of Christ. Kissing the altar was frequently connected with the presence of relics of the martyrs in altars. The Maronite (Catholic) liturgy provides a priestly farewell to the altar at the conclusion of Mass which is very beautiful and quite moving.

The notion that the priest kisses the altar which symbolizes the Church as his bride is a momentarily nice thought, but it's more trouble than it's worth. Such theology tends to become quite convoluted (consider Eastern Catholic married priests and former Anglican married clergy now functioning in the Catholic Church). I'd stick to the main idea: the priest kissing the altar is greeting Christ and all he represents.

Does the Penitential Rite at Mass Forgive Sins?

Question: *Our pastor said that our sins are forgiven at the penitential rite at the beginning of Mass? Why do we need to go to confession then?*

Answer: What are called venial or lesser sins are forgiven in a whole variety of ways, including the penitential rite at Mass. The *Catechism of the Catholic Church* makes the connection between the Eucharist and penance as follows: "Daily conversion and penance find their source and nourishment in the Eucharist, for in it is made present the sacrifice of Christ which has reconciled us with God. Through the Eucharist those who live from the life of Christ are fed and strengthened. 'It is a remedy to free us from our daily faults and to preserve us from mortal sins' " (no. 1436). Confession is a privileged way, though only one of many ways, of receiving forgiveness for venial sins.

However, the *Catechism* states, sacramental confession remains "the only ordinary way for the faithful to reconcile themselves with God and the Church" when they find themselves in serious or mortal sin (no. 1484). The penitential rite at Mass is not meant to forgive mortal sins.

When the distinction between mortal and venial sin is played down and the different means by which each is handled are blurred, then confusion such as you describe results.

Sunday Readings

Question: *Please explain how the Sunday readings are chosen and what cycles A, B, and C mean? Also, what does year I and year II mean? Why is this so complicated and how is the average person expected to follow this?*

Answer: It is necessary to differentiate here between Sundays and weekdays. The church calendar assigns a three-year cycle of Scripture readings for Sundays, for which three readings are provided. The first is usually from the Old Testament, the second from the New Testament (Letters, Acts, Revelation), and the third reading is always a selection from a Gospel.

Accordingly, the same texts are read on a particular Sunday only once every three years. Each year is designated A, B, or C. 1998 follows cycle C.

For weekdays of Ordinary Time, the Church provides a two-year cycle of readings (years I and II). For these two passages are given. The first is from the Old Testament, Letters, Acts, or Revelation, and the second is taken from one of the Gospels. The weekdays of 1998 are in year II.

Actually, the system of readings is not really complicated. Just as you don't need to know how a car engine works to drive one, so the Catholic worshiper does not need to understand the mechanics of the lectionary (book of readings) to be able to hear and appreciate the Word of God. The intent of the Church is to open the riches of Scripture to worshipers as extensively as possible.

No Gloria at Mass

Question: *The only time our priest says the Gloria is at Easter and Christmas. I realize that the Gloria is not said during Lent, but then I go to other parishes at other times in the year, and the Gloria is used. What is the ruling on saying the Gloria?*

Answer: The General Instruction of the Roman Missal (1969) states: "The Gloria is sung or said on Sundays outside of Advent and Lent, on solemnities and feasts, and at solemn local celebrations" (no. 31). The practice you describe is clearly out of keeping with this regulation.

Various motivations for dropping the Gloria are operative these days. One is based on the fact that the Gloria was not (as far as we know) introduced into the Mass until about the sixth century. Its use at all Masses of a festive character, including Sundays, became widespread only in the twelfth century.

Some argue that the Mass should be as simple as possible and that the Gloria clutters up the entrance rites. Others assert that the Gloria is an impediment to local variety and creativity, and that if used too often it becomes routine. Whatever the merits of these arguments (which, in my opinion, are few), the good order of the Church requires that the liturgy be correctly celebrated and that liturgical norms be followed. The liturgy belongs to the whole people of God, not to the priest to adapt as he wishes.

Washing Hands at Mass

Question: *Why does the priest wash his hands at Mass? What* *is the history of this practice? At our parish, the priest washes his hands only during Lent. Why is that?*

Answer: Ritual washings signifying spiritual purification have a long history in biblical religion (see Mk. 7:2-5). For Christians, baptism is the great ceremonial washing. We know that by the fourth century in Antioch and Jerusalem the bishop and the priests with him at the Eucharist washed their hands as a symbolic gesture. Wells and fountains at the entrances of Christian basilicas were used for this purpose. From this practice came holy water fonts, from which people today spiritually "wash" themselves as they enter a church.

Over the centuries, the washing of the priest's hands was variously positioned, sometimes before the people brought their gifts forward, sometimes after. In 1570, Pius V placed the washing after the prayer over the gifts (or the incensation of the altar), where it remains today.

Today, the priest says inaudibly, while washing, the words from Psalm 51: "Lord, wash away my iniquity; cleanse me from my sin."

As to why your priest washes his hands only during Lent, I can only guess. It might be that he feels unworthy or sinful only during that season, but I doubt it. Certainly, the rite is a secondary one, and it should not be a big production. Still it is required, and it is good for the souls of priests at all Masses.

Washing Hands

Question: *My missal states that the priest says in silence, while washing his hands, "Lord, wash away my iniquity; cleanse me from my sin." A priest I know is in the habit of saying loudly "Lord, wash away our iniquities; cleanse us from our sins." Please comment.*

Answer: It may be that the priest is a member of some European aristocracy or royal family which would accord him a general right to use the royal "our" rather than "my." But even then, he should follow the text provided in the Sacramentary (Mass book).

The prayer in question is a private intercession of the priest. It was never a prayer said on behalf of the congregation.

Besides, turning the washing of the hands (a relatively minor part of the Mass) into a big production is not appropriate. I heard of a church where everyone came forward at Mass to wash their hands. The resulting water all over the floor unfortunately caused someone to fall. The diocesan attorney heard about it, and that was the end of that.

I've said it before and I'll say it again: priests and people should "stick to the book."

Altar Bell

Question: *Our pastor has recently brought back the altar bells for the consecration. I thought this was no longer allowed. The pastor says he wants to restore faith in the Blessed Sacrament.*

Answer: The ringing of a bell at the Holy, Holy and the elevations of the host and chalice during the consecration is an old custom. In certain countries, the bell was also rung before the communion of the priest. The practice originated, at least in part, as a means of drawing the attention of the people to the consecration at Mass. This made sense particularly when Mass was in Latin and public address systems did not exist.

While the ringing of bells is no longer prescribed by the norms for the revised liturgy, there is nothing that forbids the practice. It is not unreasonable that it continue where it has an established history.

Where bell ringing during the liturgy was discontinued when the revised Order of Mass was introduced, I see no compelling reason to bring it back now. While the aim of restoring faith in the Blessed Sacrament is a completely worthy one, I am not sure that restoring bells during the Eucharist is going to have much effect. There are many other factors that are more important: a general atmosphere of reverence on the part of priest and people, the careful and serious celebration of the rites, and good catechesis on the Eucharist, particularly on the matter of the transformation of the bread and wine into the sacrament of Christ's Body and Blood.

Sign of Peace

Question: *Medical experts say that disease comes from the hands more than any part of the body. Many people in church are coughing and sneezing into their hands. Most people I talk to do not want to shake hands.*

Answer: One can generally find a health reason for avoiding any liturgical practice one dislikes: drinking from the chalice, kneeling, receiving communion (I know someone who receives only once a year out of an inordinate fear of germs). The sign of peace also invites health objections. Certainly people should take reasonable precautions if they have health problems, and a person who has just sneezed 750,000 cold germs into his or her hands should be careful not to pass them on to others. But the fact is we live in a world of germs and of minuscule organisms of all kinds. (Has your dentist ever shown you under a microscope the armies of creatures that live in your teeth? It makes you feel like your mouth is a walking tropical jungle!) Short of going to Mass in a space suit, one can't avoid germs.

The sign of peace does have its health hazards (as does breathing). I'm the last person to encourage marathon hug-and-kiss sessions during the sign of peace, but the gesture is profoundly meaningful. When you extend your hand to another at Mass, you are greeting all humanity in that person: you are expressing solidarity with every baptized person; you are saying that your basic stance toward fellow men and women is not hostility but friendship; you are greeting Christ in your neighbor.

Think what a transformation of the world would take place if the meaning of the sign of peace were lived out in our everyday lives. Our eucharistic communion is not only with Christ, but with all our brothers and sisters in Christ.

Smiling Eucharistic Minister

Question: *In our parish, the trainer of eucharistic ministers tells us we should make eye contact with and smile at everyone to whom we give Communion. Is there a basis for this practice?*

Answer: I once heard of an English lady who complained that the thing she disliked most about the post-Vatican II liturgy is that the eucharistic ministers always "grinned" at her.

Nothing concerning faith and morals is involved here, and the church's liturgical regulations are silent on the matter you describe.

I am a firm believer in the "eye contact" approach when giving Communion to children. At our parish primary school Masses, I found myself concerned by the casualness and lack of focus with which the students approached Communion. I trained them to look me in the eye and then at the host before I actually gave them Communion. The results in eucharistic concentration and reverence were quite noticeable.

I wouldn't push this with adults. As long as they focus on the host, that, in my opinion, is the important thing. Clergy and eucharistic ministers properly distribute the Eucharist with careful, deliberate, slow gestures. I see no reason to add a smile to the proceedings. This can seem contrived and artificial. On the other hand, scowling, looking disinterested, or being mechanical is hardly appropriate. As a serious-looking guy, I try to appear reverently pleasant when giving Communion. Sustained smiling would strain my facial muscles.

The Body of Christ

Question: *I am a eucharistic minister at my parish. For a long time, I was using "This is the Body of Christ" when I was giving the host to the people. A couple of weeks ago, my pastor asked me to start using "The Body of Christ." Please clarify the Church's teaching on this.*

Answer: Your pastor is correct on this matter. The only words that may be used in the distribution of communion are "The Body of Christ." You will notice that a verb is missing. Why? Because the phrase contains many meanings: "This is the Body of Christ"; "Become the Body of Christ"; "You are a member of the Body of Christ." All these meanings are condensed in the simple words used for distribution. The words you have been using are theologically correct (if not approved). The problem is that you are selecting out one meaning and ignoring the others.

St. Augustine wrote powerfully on this theme in his sermons on the Eucharist. He explored repeatedly the many meanings of the phrase "the Body of Christ" that I have just described.

"Presence of Christ"?

Question: *Our parish was recently assigned a new pastor. When he distributes Communion at Mass he says, "The Presence of Christ" instead of, "The Body of Christ." Is this acceptable?*

Answer: I will never tire of saying that priests and people should trust the liturgy of the Church as given and avoid making unauthorized adaptations of it. There exists no protocol for substituting the words "The Presence of Christ" for the correct words "The Body of Christ." Priests who make such changes are practicing a new form of clericalism — that is, acting as though the liturgy belongs to them and not to the whole Church, including the worshiping congregation.

The fundamental problem here is not the violation of liturgical rules. It is that the priest is espousing at a practical level a weak and ambiguous theology of the Eucharist. The words "The Body of Christ" hold together many crucial elements of Catholic eucharistic faith: that the bread and wine become the Body and Blood of Christ; that the people truly receive the Body and Blood of Christ in Communion; that by eucharistic reception the people are united more fully to — and themselves become in the process — the Body and Blood of Christ.

Nearly 2,000 years of rich and profound Christian belief about the Eucharist is expressed in the simple words "The Body of Christ." Substitutions of the kind you mention are weak, unfocused, and highly ambiguous.

Receiving the Chalice

Question: *Why do some Catholic parishes give the chalice to the people nowadays? Is this allowed? What do you think of the practice?*

Answer: While Catholic belief affirms that Christ is truly received under the species of bread alone, modern liturgical renewal has emphasized the spiritual value of receiving also from the chalice. The 1969 General Instruction of the Roman Missal states: "The sign of communion is more complete when given under both kinds, since in that form the sign of the eucharistic meal appears more clearly. The intention of Christ that the new and eternal covenant be ratified in his blood is better expressed, as is the relation of the eucharistic banquet to the heavenly banquet" (no. 240).

In the United States, the distribution of the chalice to the people is permitted at all Masses, excepting situations in which reverent distribution of the chalice cannot be guaranteed (at Masses in stadiums, for instance). Not all parishes practice this option, of course.

What do I think of this practice? I am all for it, and I encourage it highly. The restoration of the chalice to the people is, in my view, one of the most valuable features of modern liturgical renewal. Think about it: the Mass in its essential elements involves prayer, the reading and proclamation of Scripture, the consecration of bread and wine, and the reception of the consecrated gifts. All else builds on these basic elements.

Catholics are, of course, free not to receive from the chalice. Those who do not receive from the cup should not, however, simply ignore it as they pass by, but should make toward it at least a mental act of reverence.

Bread and Wine at Mass
Question: *When I have attended Mass in parishes other than my own, white wine or rosé wine was used instead of the traditional red. On one of these occasions the congregation*

was also offered a choice of the traditional host or a cube of bread. What does the Church teach?

Answer: Nothing in church law requires that the wine used at Mass be red. Some people think that since red wine looks more like blood, its use is preferable to white or rosé. This is to miss the point that the blood of Christ received in the Eucharist is not akin to natural human blood, but is the blood of Christ risen from the dead and transfigured in the power of the Spirit.

The Church requires that eucharistic wine be from grapes (and not any other kind of fruit), that it be natural (that is from actual vines and not an artificial chemical product), that it be incorrupt (that is, not have turned to vinegar), and that no other substances be added (like excessive amounts of water) to such an extent that it would lose the quality of wine.

Regarding eucharistic bread, the requirement is that it be made from wheat flour and water, and not so deteriorated that it could no longer be considered bread. The use of additives (such as honey or sugar) is illicit. The physical composition of bread and wine is the fundamental issue here. The matters of shape and color are of no theological significance. Of course, the importance of not causing confusion or creating conditions for irreverence needs underlining. I can't imagine people being offered a choice of types of bread at a particular Mass (but then I can't imagine lots of things!).

Dismissal

Question: *In our parish, the priest always ends Mass by saying: "Go in peace, the Mass has just begun." Is that acceptable?*

Answer: Your pastor has a flair for the dramatic. Theologically, there is a point to what he is saying (which I hope he has explained to his parishioners). The Dismissal Rite at the end of Mass sends us forth to put into practice what we have proclaimed and enacted in the Eucharist. Form C of the Dismissal Rite ("Go in peace to love and serve the Lord") makes it clear that all are sent forth to "live the Mass," so to speak. Your pastor is correct in wanting to underline this feature of the liturgy. The Dismissal Rite is, in this respect, far more important than many people think. Indeed (according to one theory), when Mass was in Latin, the words used for the dismissal ("*Ite Missa est*") provided the very name for the Mass, "*Missa.*"

The importance of the Dismissal Rite and its real meaning are best explained in homilies and other instructions. Using unauthorized words at the end of Mass goes against the integrity of the liturgy and, in this case, can be confusing and is apt to become tiresome.

Requiem Mass

Question: *I am confused as to what to call a funeral Mass these days: a Requiem Mass or a Mass of the Resurrection. Which is correct? My pastor told us we cannot use the term "Requiem Mass" anymore.*

Answer: While the term "Mass of the Resurrection" is popularly used for funeral Masses (and is popular among funeral directors), it is not an accurate designation. The title "Mass of the Resurrection" belongs to the Easter Vigil Eucharist.

The term "Requiem" is derived from the first word of the opening antiphon in the Latin rite funeral Mass prior to post-Vatican II revisions, which began with the words *Requiem aeternam dona eis, Domine* ("Give them eternal rest, O Lord"). Since this text is still included among the texts (in English) that may be used at the beginning of the funeral liturgy today (but is rarely heard, unfortunately), one may still correctly speak of a "Requiem Mass" (an "Eternal Rest Mass" doesn't sound quite right).

To be completely correct the term to use is "Funeral Mass." But I wouldn't go to the stake defending propriety in matters like this.

Pall

Question: *Why is the casket at funerals covered with a white cloth? Why is it called a "pall"? What is the origin and meaning of this practice.*

Answer: The term "pall" refers to a cloak or sacred covering. The funeral pall derives from the white garment that a child or adult traditionally receives at baptism. Placed over the casket at funeral Masses, the pall states that death is the completion of baptism, the definitive moment when we are called to be finally conformed to Christ.

The 1970 Order of Funerals contains the words, "On the day of his/her baptism, N. put on Christ. In the day of Christ's coming, may he/she be clothed with glory." Regrettably, in my view, these words were dropped in the 1989 revised text.

In the Book of Revelation, the saints appear in white robes that are the symbol of Christian perfection: "Then one of the elders addressed me, saying, 'Who are these people all dressed in white, and whence have they come?' I said to him, 'Sir, you know.' And he said to me, 'These are the ones who have come out of the great tribulation; they have washed their robes and made them white in the blood of the Lamb'" (Rev 7:13-14).

For the Living?

Question: *These days you hear that funerals are for the living and not the dead. This bothers me and seems to play down* *the idea of funerals as helping the dead. What is your opinion?*

Answer: My opinion is that you are right to be bothered. Certainly funerals serve a purpose for the living (but psychological counseling can probably handle this aspect of things more effectively — though "Irish" wakes are cheaper!). Probably a certain sort of reaction against the high drama of pre-Vatican II funeral liturgies has caused clergy and people to approach funerals today in a somewhat more casual manner.

The truth, however, is that funerals are for both the living and the dead. Funerals exist to commend the deceased to the providence of God and to accompany them on the way to salvation.

The *Catechism of the Catholic Church* has a powerful paragraph on the efficacy of funerals for the dead:

"The Church who, as Mother, has borne the Christian sacramentally in her womb during his earthly pilgrimage, accompanies him at his journey's end, in order to surrender him 'into the Father's hands.' She offers to the Father, in Christ, the child of his grace, and she commits to the earth, in hope, the seed of the body that will rise in glory. This offering is fully celebrated in the Eucharistic sacrifice" (no. 1683).

Funerals for Non-Catholics
Question: *Recently a non-Catholic was given a funeral at our parish church. Is this practice allowed?*

Answer: Catholic funerals may be granted in certain circumstances to baptized persons belonging to a non-Catholic church with the permission of the bishop (see Code of Canon Law 1183). A precondition is that conducting such a funeral be consistent with the general wishes and outlook of the deceased. It would be unseemly to force a Catholic funeral on someone who wouldn't want to be caught dead in a Catholic church!

Canon Law requires that the deceased have no adequate access to his or her own minister. There may, for instance, be no church or minister of the particular denomination in the area. The non-Catholic may also have stopped practicing his or her faith. A request from a Catholic spouse or next of kin would in such circumstances generally justify a Catholic funeral.

This permission cannot be granted to those who were unbaptized, although there is nothing to stop a priest or deacon providing some simple ceremony or blessing at a mortuary or graveside.

Catholic Funerals

Question: *How is it that Sonny Bono, who was married four times, and Michael Kennedy, a pro-abortion advocate, received church funerals?*

Answer: According to Canon Law, the Church denies funeral rites to certain categories of people: first, notorious apostates, heretics, and schismatics; second, those who have chosen cremation for reasons opposed to Christian faith; third, manifest sinners for whom ecclesiastical funeral rites could not be granted without public scandal (Canon 1184).

The first two categories involve people who obviously would not wish to have a Catholic funeral. The third category is more complex. The typical example is the high-profile Mafia figure whose whole moral code was at odds with Christian faith right up to the end.

The Church prefaces its legislation on this matter in

Canon 1184 with the proviso: "Unless they have given some signs of repentance before their death," the categories mentioned are to be deprived of funeral rites. The Church, reflecting the mercy of Christ, tends toward leniency in the matter of providing Christian burial. In many situations, denying ecclesiastical rites would be a source of even greater scandal than providing them.

In this matter, it is crucial that Catholics and others understand that funeral rites do not exist to honor, praise, or grant a seal of approval to the deceased (which is why tributes and eulogies are discouraged), but to commend frail and imperfect humanity to the mercy of God.

Frank Sinatra's Funeral

Question: *How could Frank Sinatra's funeral be in the Church with a Mass? They would not bury my brother from the Catholic Church when he passed away.*

Answer: Canon 1184 of the Code of Canon Law states that, "Unless they have given some signs of repentance before their death," three categories of people may be deprived of funeral rites.

As I've said, the Church, reflecting the mercy of Christ, tends toward leniency in the matter of providing Christian burial. The provision of a Catholic funeral to Frank Sinatra apparently met at least the minimal requirements for a Church funeral.

You do not state the reason your brother was not given a Catholic funeral. I can only say that the general policy of pastors is to give the benefit of the doubt in individual cases and to act in the interests of mercy and compassion. Any other policy is out of keeping with the better traditions of Catholicism.

Songs at Funerals

Question: *At a funeral the other day the offertory hymn was "My Way." The deceased was a fan of Frank Sinatra. Why is this not OK?*

Answer: Your assumption that it's not OK is well founded. First, secular songs don't belong in the liturgy because the sentiments generally don't fit. Not being familiar with all the words of the Sinatra song (and I am not about to do any significant research on the matter), the song strikes me as highly individualistic, self-focused, and blustering.

Christians do not appropriately boast about doing things "their way." Believers do things Christ's way — which is the only way to true selfhood. If we all did things "our way," we would stay dead as doornails after we draw our last breath. We can't raise ourselves from the dead; only God can. So God's way offers us the better deal.

SIX
Morality

Corporal Works of Mercy

Question: *How come no one mentions the corporal works of mercy anymore? Do they still apply?*

Answer: That the corporal works of mercy are not often referred to today according to the traditional list is certainly true. But they are certainly mentioned in other terms.

Do they still apply? Is the pope still Catholic? They are of the essence of Christian faith and provide the criteria for the Last Judgment (see Matthew 5:3-10).

The corporal works of mercy are: to feed the hungry; to give drink to the thirsty; to clothe the naked; to shelter the homeless; to visit the sick; to visit those in prison; to bury the dead.

Since Vatican II there has been in Catholicism a great and admirable emphasis on social justice, expressed in numerous ecclesiastical documents and many new and intensified initiatives at local, national and international levels. The corporal works of mercy are central to any program of Christian charity and justice. They have found admirable expression in the apostolates of people like Mother Teresa of Calcutta.

Spiritual Works of Mercy

Question: *Does the Catholic Church still hold the notion of spiritual works of mercy?*

Answer: Most certainly it does. While the term (a perfectly good and commendable one) is not familiar to many Catholics today, it serves as a memorable summary of the traditional seven forms of spiritual charity toward one's neighbors. (In contrast, the corporal works of mercy minister to people's material needs.)

The seven spiritual works of mercy are: converting the

sinner; instructing the ignorant; counseling the doubtful; comforting the sorrowful; bearing wrongs patiently; forgiving injuries; and praying for the living and the dead.

To some people, the first three can sound a little arrogant and self-righteous. But if understood correctly, they are not. The best means of "converting the sinner" is to show compassion and give good example. "Instructing the ignorant" only occurs effectively through wisdom, patience, and genuine respect. "Counseling the doubtful" is best achieved by standing in solidarity with others in their moments of confusion and bafflement.

The bases of the spiritual and corporal works of mercy are the teachings of Christ and the practice of the Church as Christ's living Body. Without these works, Christianity would be an empty shell.

Occasion of Sin?

Question: *What is meant by an occasion of sin? Does the Church have an official list? Is television an occasion of sin?*

Answer: An occasion of sin is any place, situation, or environment which predictably encourages sinful behavior. A theater specializing in X-rated material is an obvious example. Few people would leave such an establishment with their virtue fully intact.

Occasions of sin vary from person to person. One can predict, for instance, that getting together with a particular combination of people will inevitably lead to gossip, malicious talk, and generally negative conversation.

Ask yourself this question: In what circumstances or under what conditions do I find my major sins recurring? Your answer will tell you what are the major occasions of sin for you personally.

The Church does not (wisely) have an official list of occasions of sin. Television (like alcohol or a deck of cards) is not intrinsically an occasion of sin. It is morally neutral. I assume that even Mother Teresa of Calcutta had a television around somewhere.

Television can, of course, be the occasion of numerous sins: not just lust (which is what most people think of at once), but laziness, irresponsibility, neglect of spouse and children, mindlessness. On the other hand, television does provide some important cultural services: like broadcasting professional wrestling.

Near Occasions

Question: *I am a female who is attracted to my own sex. I live a chaste life, daily struggling to keep my mind and heart pure, offering my suffering to God. I have occasionally watched the TV show "Ellen," and read that her character will "come out" as a lesbian. Will it be sinful for me to continue watching the show?*

Answer: There are two aspects to your question. The first has to do with the morality of viewing ethically ambiguous presentations on TV (or in the theater). Since it is the nature of drama to portray the complexities and evils of life, the question arises: Should Christians avoid dramatic works that portray immoral situations?

Hardly. If such avoidance were morally required, Shakespeare and any great playwright would be out of bounds. It was Cardinal John Henry Newman, I think, who said that in a sinful world there is no sinless literature.

The second aspect of your question has to do with the effects upon the viewer of programs that might cause one to lapse from one's moral commitments. What have been traditionally called "occasions of sin" are properly avoided. You have to trust your judgment in choosing the kind of TV programs you watch.

If the program you mention has some meritorious value in exploring a human situation (or is merely entertaining) and does not affect you morally for the worse, there is no great objection. But if the program is likely to trouble you morally, then it is best avoided.

Forgiveness

Question: *How do you forgive someone you hate? If that person has done nothing but horrible things to you (which happened to me as a child) and you can't see any good in them. How should you handle that as a Christian?*

Answer: First, it is crucial that you take the appropriate practical steps when you are suffering from an experience of the sort you mention: Talk to your pastor or a good spiritual director; discuss matters with a wise family member or friend; or get counseling from a medical professional with a Christian perspective.

Second, pray for the person in question. This is not only good for the person for whom you are praying, but it softens the heart, making one able to understand the crosses the other person may have to carry and rendering life a little more bearable for oneself.

Some time ago I came across a striking prayer that was found near a child's body in Ravensbruch Women's Concentration Camp during World War II that I commend to you: "O Lord, remember not only the men and women of good will, but also those of evil will. But do not remember all the suffering they have inflicted upon us, Lord; remember the fruits we have bought, thanks to this suffering: our comradeship, our loyalty, our humility, our courage, our generosity, O Lord, the greatness of heart which has grown out of all this; and when they come to judgment, let all the fruits we have borne be their forgiveness."

Loving Hurtful People

Question: *I know I am supposed to love everyone. But I have a difficult time loving a member of my family who does a lot of damage and has hurt a lot of people.*

Answer: C.S. Lewis wrote a marvelous book called *The Four Loves* (published in 1960 and still in print). Lewis identified four kinds of love: affection, friendship, eros (sexual love), and charity.

Affection one can have for a little baby (or one's cat). Friendship involves a communion of heart and soul. Eros is what draws the sexes together. These are generally "easier" and more pleasant loves, though their consequences may be quite complicated.

However, the fourth kind of love, charity, can be very difficult and even unpleasant. St. Paul offers a good approach to the practice of charitable love: "Love is patient and kind. Love is not jealous or boastful; it is not arrogant or rude. Love does not insist on its own way; it is not irritable or resentful; it does not rejoice at wrong but rejoices in the right. Love bears all things, believes all things, hopes all things, endures all things" (1 Cor 13:4-7).

There are a whole series of "nots" in this kind of love. Sometimes one can love by "not" doing things. Not being rude to a hurtful person is a genuine expression of charity.

One surely cannot have either affection or friendship for

people who cause a lot of damage and hurt. Unless one is involved in what therapists call a "dysfunctional" relationship, one can hardly be sexually drawn to a consistently hurtful person. Charity is the kind of love one practices in the circumstances you describe.

Situation Ethics

Question: *What are "situation ethics?" Can Catholics believe in them? I am told some Catholic theologians teach situation ethics.*

Answer: Situation ethics is a system of morality made popular by the publication of the book *Situation Ethics* by Episcopalian theologian Joseph Fletcher in 1966. Situation ethics does not recognize the existence of universal moral norms. It holds that every moral situation is unique and unrepeatable and that when the individual follows his or her conscience in a particular situation, then he or she has acted morally. As long as the person is sincere and believes himself or herself to be acting in good faith — and the results of the action are not unjust or damaging to others — then no other overriding considerations apply. Situationism is very widespread in present-day American culture. Much television talk-show morality is in this vein.

In 1952, Pope Piux XII condemned situation ethics, a position the Church has not revised. Since Christ and the Church teach the existence of objective, binding, and irreversible moral norms, it is not possible to see how a Catholic could practice situation ethics.

While certain notions found in situation ethics are present in the thought of some Catholic moral theologians, I know of no prominent Catholic moralist who espouses anything close to full-fledged situation ethics.

Hate Over Abortion

Question: *A girl I used to be best friends with recently had an abortion. Now, every time I look at her it makes me furious and extremely sad. How do I handle these emotions? I'm afraid my hate of her sin is being mistaken for hate of her.*

Answer: The admonition to "love the sinner, but hate the sin" is easier said than done. On the one hand, we are required to stand by our moral principles; on the other, we are called to be compassionate and loving of those who fail to live up to the Gospel. The mixed and confused emotions you experience are perfectly natural, and there is no easy solution to them.

One way to try to handle the matter is by intense prayer for your friend. Prayer is not only good for your friend, but it will also soften your own heart and keep you from bitterness and destructive emotions. In prayer, you can try to see your friend with the "eyes" of God and to understand what pressures may have been working upon her. In prayer, you can ask for yourself something of the compassion of God. Beyond this, it would be appropriate to communicate to your friend that while you cannot approve of what she has done, you are there to help her should she need you.

Abortion

Question: *What should you say to someone you know who has had an abortion, so that you are merciful without approving her action?*

Answer: I can think of no better answer than that provided by Pope John Paul II in his 1995 encyclical entitled "The Gospel of Life" *(Evangelium Vitae)*. The quotation is longish but worth every word.

The Pope writes: "I would now like to say a special word

to women who have had an abortion. The Church is aware of the many factors which may have influenced your decision, and she does not doubt that in many cases it was a painful and even shattering decision. The wound in your heart may not yet have healed. Certainly what happened was and remains terribly wrong. But do not give in to discouragement and do not lose hope. Try rather to understand what happened and face it honestly. If you have not already done so, give yourselves over with humility and trust to repentance. The Father of mercies is ready to give you his forgiveness and his peace in the Sacrament of Reconciliation. You will come to understand that nothing is definitively lost and you will also be able to ask forgiveness from your child, who is now living in the Lord. With the friendly and expert help and advice of other people, and as a result of your own painful experience, you can be among the most eloquent defenders of everyone's right to life. Through your commitment to life, whether by accepting the birth of other children or by welcoming and caring for those most in need of someone to be close to them, you will become promoters of a new way of looking at human life" (no. 99).

Living Together

Question: *My niece's ex-husband is seeking an annulment in order to remarry. He and his fiancée are living together. His priest said that it was permissible for them to have sex, since they will be getting married eventually. Is this true?*

Answer: A pastor who would give the advice you mention is not being faithful to Catholic moral theology or authentic pastoral practice. Your question raises the whole matter of why the Church opposes "living together." The Church here is not simply being prudish, old-fashioned, or a spoil-sport.

Catholic morality is not arbitrary, but is based on a combination of divine revelation and accumulated human wisdom.

The problem with "living together" before marriage is that the practice is neither good for sexuality nor for marriage. By "living together" people disconnect sexuality from marriage and from a life-long covenant of love. Cohabitating couples tend to carry the same casualness and lack of commitment into marriage. Those people who "live together" before marriage tend to stay "living together" after marriage! Not surprisingly many get divorced.

There is a growing body of studies that indicate the problematic features of cohabitating before marriage. The modern wisdom that "living together" is a good idea and leads to more stable marriages is, in fact, contradicted by some very substantive social-scientific evidence.

Fertility Drugs

Question: *What does the Church think about fertility drugs? When is it acceptable to use them?*

Answer: The Church's position on the question of fertility is available in a 1987 document from the Vatican Congregation for the Doctrine of the Faith entitled "Instruction on Respect for Human Life in Its Origins and on the Dignity of Procreation" (*Donum Vitae*). It is also summarized in the *Catechism of the Catholic Church* (nos. 2373-2379).

In general, the Church encourages and promotes research into the problem of human infertility and sterility. However, it regards as unacceptable any techniques that involve the separation of husband and wife from the act of procreation — for example, the donation of sperm or ovum or the use of a surrogate womb.

In respect to techniques involving the married couple —

for example, artificial insemination of the husband's sperm — the *Catechism* says such techniques "are perhaps less reprehensible, yet remain morally unacceptable. They dissociate the sexual act from the procreative act" (no. 2377).

While the procedures described are frowned upon by the Church, taking drugs to enhance fertility in a responsible and medically sound manner is morally acceptable. In this situation, the processes of nature are being enhanced but not interfered with and the integrity of the relationship between husband and wife is respected.

Death Penalty

Question: *Someone told me that the Church has changed its teaching on the death penalty in the very latest edition of the* Catechism of the Catholic Church. *Is this true?*

Answer: Whenever you hear that "the Church has changed its teaching" you should be suspicious. The Church may modify what does not belong to the substance of faith, but does not change its fundamental teaching.

In the case of the death penalty, the Church has always held that, for the protection of society, the state lawfully may have recourse to the death penalty to repel an unjust aggressor if no other means are available. This teaching is repeated in nos. 2265-2267 of the *Catechism of the Catholic Church*, issued in 1992.

The application of this teaching may, however, change from situation to situation. The Latin (and definitive) version of the new *Catechism* published last year tightens up the circumstances in which the state nowadays may legitimately have recourse to the death penalty. Here the *Catechism* is reflecting the teaching of Pope John Paul II in his 1995 encyclical *Evangelium Vitae*.

The key paragraph inserted into the 1997 Latin text is the following one: "Today, in fact, given the means at the state's disposal effectively to repress crime by rendering inoffensive the one who has committed it, without depriving him definitively of the possibility of redeeming himself, cases of absolute necessity for suppression of the offender today 'are very rare, if not practically non-existent' (*Evangelium Vitae*, no. 56)." In short, the Church increasingly envisages few social or political circumstances in which the death penalty is justified.

Nude Ecclesiastical Art

Question: *What is the proper thinking on nude ecclesiastical art? My husband says that "some church art is just a hair away from pornography."*

Answer: It is unlikely that we will see a new flourishing of nude art in Catholic churches any time soon. During the Renaissance era in particular, however, there existed a great fascination with the human body. Consider Michelangelo's work!

The human body is, after all, God's creation. Pope John Paul II has explored this theme extensively. What we do with the body and how we view it determines whether our approach is moral or immoral.

Artistic depictions of the body which explore the grandness, nobility, and beauty of the human person are perfectly appropriate. (If not, the pope needs to whitewash the Sistine Chapel.) Pornography, on the other hand, means the depiction of the human body for degrading and base purposes. The word "pornography" literally means "the writing of harlots." Nude art designed to exploit sexuality is covered by this description.

Cultural sensitivities make a big difference on this matter.

It is amusing to observe a group of Americans viewing Michelangelo's famous "David" in Florence. Everyone watches the other to see how he or she is reacting. Italians, by contrast, are not at all uncomfortable with nude statuary. Consider, too, that, in one perspective, all of us are nudes with clothes on — not, I caution, a line of thought to be entertained in church during a boring homily.

Biorhythm

Question: *My sister regularly goes to the hospital for bio-feedback. The whole thing sounds a little suspect to me. Does the Church approve of this? What is your opinion?*

Answer: You are addressing your question to someone who is as thick as a brick when it comes to medicine or technology — anything remotely connected to science or machinery (I barely know how to put gas in my car). Biorhythmic feedback, as explained to me by a medical technologist (albeit at a cocktail party), has to do with the monitoring of biological rhythms and their connection to psychological states for the purpose of producing a calmer and less stressful mode of daily living.

Apparently there exist regular cycles of biological change in the human person connected to his or her temperament and physical condition. These cycles affect a person's emotional and mental states. Their adverse results can be controlled somewhat by careful monitoring and retraining of the mind-body connection.

As long as biorhythmic feedback procedures do not alter a person's mental clarity or sense of moral responsibility (alterations, I am told, that do not generally occur), the Church would have no objections. If your sister is positively helped by bio-feedback, then you should not discourage her from continuing treatment — everyone remaining mindful, of course, that there are no quick fixes in life.

Morality of Music

Question: *Our pastor recently gave a sermon about the bad effects of the MTV cable channel on young people. He said certain kinds of music are automatically immoral. What do you think?*

Answer: As an occasional viewer of MTV (for the purposes of self-education, you understand), the channel has, in my judgment, almost nothing going for it, and its effects on young people who are too easily impressed or lacking in discernment would range from questionable to atrocious.

MTV is not genuinely cutting-edge, daring, or avant-garde. It's just mind-numbingly stupid. It's trash TV for teenagers. It makes Jerry Springer look like William Buckley. Your pastor was probably on the right track. (Am I making myself clear?)

Music can be immoral in two ways. First, in its lyrics. Words which express or encourage immoral thoughts or actions are in themselves immoral. For instance, MTV-type lyrics (I'm using "lyric" loosely), habitually demean women, ethnic groups, and indeed the human race in general.

Second, apart from words, music has an ability to generate both noble and base emotions. Plato distinguished between Appolonian and Dionysian types of music. The former (more melodic than rhythmic) tends to generate personal composure and self-possession. The latter (more rhythmic than melodic) encourages excited and energetic mental and physical states.

One shouldn't take this distinction to extremes. Musicologists do, however, continue to hold that something inherent in certain musical patterns produces predictable human responses, either positive or negative.

Servile Work

Question: *Is it okay to wash cars on Sunday? When I was young it was forbidden as "servile work." Now everyone is doing it.*

Answer: I'm one of those people who (to the puzzlement of gas station attendants) always passes up the chance of a free car wash with a fill-up. Life is just too short! Some people seem to enjoy actually washing their cars (which I cannot imagine), so for them such activity belongs in the category of recreation. Accordingly, it need not belong in the category of "servile work" traditionally forbidden by the Church.

Servile work meant the heavy labor of serfs, from which they were freed on Sundays and holy days. Servile work was prohibited for a purpose: to ensure the possibility of attendance at worship.

The *Catechism of the Catholic Church* spells out well the meaning of Sunday as a day of rest: "On Sundays and other holy days of obligation, the faithful are to refrain from engaging in work or activities that hinder the worship owed to God, the joy proper to the Lord's Day, the performance of the works of mercy, and the appropriate relaxation of mind and body. Family needs or important social service can legitimately excuse from the obligation of Sunday rest. The faithful should see to it that legitimate excuses do not lead to habits prejudicial to religion, family life, and health" (no. 2185).

Good works for others and personal growth are especially important on Sundays. The *Catechism* continues: "Sunday is traditionally consecrated by Christian piety to good works and humble service of the sick, the infirm, and the elderly. Christians will also sanctify Sunday by devoting time and care to their families and relatives, often difficult to do on other days of the week. Sunday is a time for reflection, silence, cultivation of the mind, and meditation which furthers the growth of the Christian interior life" (no. 2186).

In his Pentecost Sunday Apostolic Letter of 1997, "On Keeping the Lord's Day" (*Dies Domini*), Pope John Paul II called Catholics to a comprehensive renewal of their sense of the priority of Sunday as a day of worship, rest, and service.

Are Bingo and Raffles Immoral?

Question: *I remember reading somewhere that the Church discourages games of chance for raising funds. Could you please enlighten me on this and cite some teachings of the Church I could present to our parish?*

Answer: The Church does not encourage gambling, raffles, or what are nicely known as "games of chance." But neither are they forbidden.

The *Catechism of the Catholic Church* treats the matter under the Seventh Commandment, "You shall not steal."

This commandment forbids unjustly taking or keeping the goods of others and wronging one's neighbors with respect to their property. Positively, it encourages justice, charity, and the sharing of material resources.

The *Catechism* states: "*Games of chance* (card games, etc.) or *wagers* are not in themselves contrary to justice. They become morally unacceptable when they deprive someone of what is necessary to provide for his needs and those of others. The passion for gambling risks becoming an enslavement" (no. 2413). Unfair wagers and cheating are, of course, immoral.

Raffles, bingos, and gambling do not, in my opinion, constitute the best means for parochial fund-raising. (In some places, such activities are illegal.)

I propose the following guidelines: games of chance should be used in parishes only for unambiguously good causes (for example, feeding the poor, not for a new bar in the rectory); they should be used sparingly; so that they do not discourage a sense of parochial stewardship; vigilance about abuses is necessary (if a poor family buys $300 worth of raffle tickets, someone should check out the situation); prudence and good sense should prevail so that people are not shocked by the perception that the parish hall is turning into a gambling joint.

The Holocaust

Question: *I heard that the Church was working on a document on the Holocaust. As a Jewish convert, I wonder why is it so difficult for the Church to denounce the Holocaust.*

Answer: Recent popes and numerous church agencies have, in fact, denounced the Holocaust. The present pope has spoken very passionately on the matter. In a homily delivered in 1979, Pope John Paul called Auschwitz the "Golgotha of the modern world." In an apostolic letter on the fiftieth anniversary of the beginning of World War II, the pope stressed the uniqueness of the Jewish suffering, which, he said, "will forever remain a shame for humanity." An important collection of Pope John Paul's addresses, "On Jews and Judaism 1979-1986," was published in 1987, leaving no doubt that the Holocaust is a dominant concern of the present pope's consciousness.

A definitive statement on the Holocaust was published by the Vatican in 1998 entitled, "We Remember: A Reflection on the Shoah." The document describes the Holocaust as an "unspeakable tragedy, which can never be forgotten" and it deplores the attempted extermination of the Jewish people:

"The inhumanity with which the Jews were persecuted and massacred during this century is beyond the capacity of words to convey."

The document recognizes that "The history of relations between Jews and Christians is a tormented one." It expresses the "deep sorrow" of the Catholic Church for the failures of its people in this matter. It concludes: "The spoiled seeds of anti-Judaism and anti-Semitism must never again be allowed to take root in any human heart."

SEVEN

Catholic Practices and Devotions

Prayer
Saints
Symbols
Sacramentals
Devotions
Shrines
Movements
Media
Burial

Morning Offering

Question: *When I was young we said the Morning Offering at home every day. Can you refresh me on the words? Where did they come from? Are they still valid?*

Answer: The Morning Offering is a prayer for the dedication of the entire day to the Sacred Heart of Jesus. It originated with the Apostleship of Prayer (League of the Sacred Heart), whose statutes were approved by the Holy See in 1879.

The prayer reads: "O Jesus, through the immaculate heart of Mary I offer You all my prayers, works, joys, and sufferings of this day for all the intentions of Your Sacred Heart, in union with the holy sacrifice of the Mass throughout the world, in reparation for my sins, for the intentions of all our associates, and in particular for the intentions of the Holy Father."

This prayer (which exists in a number of versions) can serve as a very effective means of seeing one's day in the context of eternity, of regarding daily circumstances as opportunities for grace and, not least, of integrating prayer and work. The traditional version lends itself to personal adaptation.

Certainly, the Morning Offering is still valid. Even if one does not use the exact words or even makes up one's own, the idea of dedicating each day in its totality to God is highly commendable.

Liturgy of the Hours

Question: *I know lay people who are saying the Liturgy of the Hours or what used to be called the Divine Office. Is this allowed by the Church? Where would I begin?*

Answer: Allowed! It's enthusiastically encouraged! The Constitution on the Sacred Liturgy of Vatican II stated: "The laity, too, are encouraged to recite the divine office, either with the priests, or among themselves, or even individually" (no. 100).

When the vernacular version of the revised Liturgy of the Hours came out in the mid-1970s, there was great hope that the laity would take up the recitation of the Hours. This has not, unfortunately, happened to the degree hoped for — though there are, I would guess, at least a few laity in every parish who recite the Hours on a regular basis.

The Liturgy of the Hours can seem very complicated to the beginner. Where should one begin? First, obtain a version that has at least morning and evening prayer (check with your local Catholic bookstore). Then ask your parish priest how to use the office. He may know someone in the parish who is already saying the Liturgy of the Hours who could help you.

Parish groups saying the Hours before or after morning or evening Mass is a highly commendable practice. If you find others in the parish who would wish to say the Liturgy of the Hours communally, then ask the pastor if you could pray the Hours together in the church. Most pastors would be delighted at such a prospect.

Dryness in Prayer

Question: *As a 22-year-old Catholic, I try to take my faith seriously and pray every day. Lately, I find prayer very difficult and dry. Do you have any suggestions?*

Answer: If you find prayer difficult, you are in good company. Some of the great saints struggled with aridity of soul and spirit. St. John of the Cross's description of the "dark night of the soul" finds some resonance in many of us regularly.

What St. Paul writes in his Letter to the Romans is very helpful with the difficulty you describe: "Likewise the Spirit too helps us in our weakness; for we do not know how to pray as we ought; but the Spirit himself intercedes for us with sighs too deep for words. And he who searches the hearts of men knows what is the mind of the Spirit, because the Spirit intercedes for the saints according to the will of God" (8:26-27).

Periods when we find prayer a chore sometimes result from trying too hard to pray. The more we go on spiritual overdrive, the less successful is the outcome. It is best to stop and let God pray in and through us. We can simply sit or kneel quietly, place ourselves in the presence of God, and ask the Holy Spirit to move in our hearts and be our advocate.

The communion of saints is also important in times of spiritual dryness. When we are unable to pray, we can have recourse to the aid of the saints, slowly going through the Litany of the Saints, for example, asking each saint to "pray for us." The saints pray on our behalf when we ourselves are unable to do so.

Distraction During Prayer

Question: *When I pray the rosary, my mind wanders. I have used the scriptural rosary, which helps to keep my mind focused but this does not always work. Do you have any suggestions for this problem?*

Answer: Distraction during prayer is as old as prayer itself. I suggest a couple of strategies. The first is not to fight distraction too much. Distractions during prayers are like bees during a summer walk. The more you fight them, the more they come after you. Second, you can turn your distraction into prayer. Ask God's wisdom about the matter that is distracting you. If you are distracted by something that is bothering or irritating you, stop and pray for the gift of patience and understanding regarding the situation. You can turn matters that distract you into occasions for intercession and meditation. Thankfully, God understands the processes of your heart, and it does not matter to him that your rosary is disorganized and beset by fits and starts.

Third, you may want to shorten your prayers, particularly on occasions when you are especially distracted. A few minutes of concentrated prayer beats an hour of floundering around with more prayers than you can manage at the moment.

Centering Prayer

Question: *I hear a lot of talk these days about "centering prayer." Please explain what it is and if it is good for us.*

Answer: Centering prayer is one of many forms of contemplative prayer. Among its roots are the reflective mode of reading the Bible called "*lectio divina*" associated with monastic life. St. Gregory the Great spoke of a kind of prayer that is a quiet "resting in God." Centering prayer has been made popular in recent times by Cistercian monks Thomas Keating and Basil Pennington.

Typically, centering prayer means assuming a still posture, closing one's eyes, and focusing on the presence and action of God in one's heart. I once had the privilege of seeing Pope John Paul at close quarters in a state of deep contemplation before Mass. The Pope's mode of prayer, by which the Eucharist and the word of God are invited into the very center of one's being, is a model of centering prayer.

There also exists a New Age type of centering prayer. One sits quietly and calmly letting the God within the self — indeed the God who is the self — well up and overflow into one's emotions and feelings. Here the individual's own spiritual center is regarded as God.

In Christian centering prayer, one centers oneself in Christ and the sacraments. In New Age centering prayer, self-centeredness is the principal goal.

Failure-Proof Prayers

Question: *A prayer called "Prayer to the Blessed Virgin" appears from time to time in the ads section of a local newspaper. It is described as "never known to fail." After three days of saying it we are supposed to publish it somewhere. I admit to a little skepticism. Your response, please.*

Answer: Those who promote such prayers are generally men and women of faith and goodwill. We should avoid a dismissive attitude toward them. However, such prayers do not represent the best understanding of what intercession is about.

There are at least two ways to approach prayer: as a communication of love and trust, and as a businesslike transaction. When we pray authentically we are opening ourselves to God's will and trusting him to answer us. The answer may come in ways we do not expect. We cannot predict or manipulate God. In that God always answers our pleas in one way or another, there is truth in the claim that authentic prayers are "never known to fail."

However, prayers that involve strict formulas, mathematics, and requirements for publication or dissemination represent an impoverished approach to the spiritual life. We should never approach prayer as if conducting a business transaction with God.

Prayer for Souls in Purgatory

Question: *Our Lord told St. Gertrude that a certain prayer which he dictated to her would release 1,000 souls from purgatory each time it is said. Is this true?*

Answer: The prayer you mention and the story accompanying it belong in the category of private revelation. For this reason, Catholics are not required to believe in them. Such revelations and the devotions they foster are to be judged by their consistency with Catholic tradition.

Is intercession for the souls in purgatory a good thing? Certainly. Is prayer to God very powerful? Absolutely. Accordingly, in these regards the prayer of St. Gertrude is consistent with Catholic faith.

What should one make of the number 1,000 in the prayer? I suggest that it is a symbolic number meaning "many souls." Nothing in official Catholic teaching allows us to state that God grants definite and calculable answers to prayers. It is always necessary for us to extract the essential points of private revelations from their symbolic or visionary dressing.

Catholics are not wise to give undue credence to every detail of such revelations, but neither are we wise to be merely skeptical and dismissive. We should always search for what is good and edifying in revelations of the kind you mention.

Healing Family Trees

Question: *A Prayer for Healing the Family Tree includes the following: "Heavenly Father . . . I ask you to forgive the sins of my ancestors whose failures have left their effects on me in unwanted tendencies, behavior patterns and defects in body, mind and spirit. . . . I symbolically place the Cross of Jesus over the head of each person in my family tree, and between each generation; I ask you to let the cleansing blood of Jesus purify the bloodlines in my family lineage." Please comment.*

Answer: The author appears to be reinventing the wheel. Prayers to and for one's ancestors, for the souls in purgatory, offering to and asking forgiveness from the dead, are all perfectly sound and commendable Catholic traditions. The language of "geneagrams," "transgenerational bondage" and the "healing of the family tree" strikes me as rather esoteric (like something one might hear on "Star Trek") and, in the light of what I just said, unnecessary.

Perhaps the author is not familiar with the richness of Catholic tradition on this matter? The prayer also seems to me a little self-centered. Placing oneself at the center of a genealogical map that extends infinitely backwards and forwards is to situate oneself unduly at the center of human history.

Steps to Sainthood

Question: *What are the official steps to sainthood? Has the church updated the process since Vatican II?*

Answer: The present canonization procedure was put in place in 1983 and involves three steps. The process begins when a local bishop in consultation with some fellow bishops decides that the virtuous life of a deceased person seems worthy of investigation. Then, based on the bishop's submission, the Vatican Congregation for the Causes of Saints researches the candidate's life further to verify if the person practiced Christian virtue to a heroic degree. The Congregation may or may not recommend the cause of the candidate to the pope. If the pope accepts a positive recommendation, the candidate is termed "venerable."

This second step builds upon the first and leads, if successful, to beatification. This involves a lengthy process of scrutiny of the person's life, character, and reputation. Customarily one miracle must be credited to the candidate's intercession with God. The candidate may then be "beatified" by the pope, thereby becoming "blessed."

The final step is canonization, at which point the person is declared "saint." For this a second miracle is required. Canonization means being "raised to the full honors of the altar" and venerated by the whole Church.

Saints and Special Favors

Question: *Why do Catholics pray to different saints for "special favors" instead of talking directly to God without "in betweens"?*

Answer: Because we live in a universe of "in betweens." Consider everyday life. None of us lives in isolation. We are not independent, self-made creatures. For life, love, truth, and happiness, and all sorts of material things, we depend on the skills, talents, commitments of others: parents, friends, neighbors, teachers, doctors. If you have a bad day, you talk to a wise friend. If you are sick, you go to the doctor. If your car transmission breaks down, you take it to the service station.

So it is within the communion of saints. Surely St. Thomas Aquinas has a special concern for theologians. St. Francis of Assisi prays for and inspires in a special way those who want to live the simple joy of the Gospel. Would not Mother Teresa of Calcutta want to help in a particular way those who serve the poor?

When we pray to special saints we do so because the particular concern or commitment such saints had in their lifetime continues after their death. Prayer to the saints "for special favors" is best not seen as a matter of greedily seeking things like a new car or a salary raise. What the saints most have to offer us is the inspiration of their lives that we may emulate their holiness and unselfish good deeds.

St. Jude

Question: *I often pray to St. Jude. How do you approach the saint of hopeless cases when you yourself are not desperate. Can you still pray to him?*

Answer: Of course you can. You can start by telling St. Jude how grateful you are that you are not desperate. There exist no restrictions on prayer to the saints as long as they are in conformity with Catholic doctrine, wholesome piety, and common sense.

On the matter of prayer to the saints, Catholics are too easily influenced by old Protestant hang-ups. The fact is the saints are part of the great Christian family spread over space and time uniting the faithful on earth with those in heaven. We can all talk freely to the members of God's saintly family. The saints do not get in our way to God; they lead us to God. Just as in our ordinary lives we exist in a great conversation of love with many others, so we can communicate with the saints in heaven in all their splendid, personal variety.

Thankfully, you may not feel desperate or hopeless; but many people in fact do. Some people have no one to love them, feel little hope in their lives, and do not know how to pray. You can intercede with St. Jude for such men and women — people you may not even know — who are desperate and hopeless. This way we can be united with our needy fellow men and women through the saints in a powerful communion of love.

St. Blase

Question: *Is the blessing of throats still allowed on the feast of St. Blase? Who was St. Blase? A CCD teacher in our parish said the blessing of throats was outdated and that we should go to the doctor instead.*

Question: *Where did the Blessing of Throats on St. Blase's Day come from? Some of my friends say it is superstitious.*

Answer: As a child, I was often irritated at Saint Blase because I suffered from regular and prolonged throat infections and found St. Blase no help whatsoever. As I grew up, I came to realize that such blessings are not miracle cures, but prayers that recognize that God is the author of all healing, including the healing provided by throat specialists. When prayers are approached superstitiously they are being abused. The Church does not encourage such an approach.

Since the 1989 official Book of Blessings provides an Order for the Blessing of Throats on the Feast of Saint Blase (February 3), the Church (unlike the CCD teacher in the first question) clearly does not regard the rite of blessing throats as outdated.

The Book of Blessings provides a brief account of St. Blase as follows: "St. Blase was the bishop of Sebaste in Armenia during the fourth century. Very little is known about his life. According to various accounts he was a physician before becoming a bishop. His cult spread throughout the entire Church in the Middle Ages because he was reputed to have miraculously cured a little boy who nearly died because of a fishbone in his throat. From the eighth century he has been invoked on behalf of the sick, especially those afflicted with illnesses of the throat" (1625).

The Blessing of Throats is not magic, but a statement of God's concern for our most ordinary human ailments. The liturgical blessing of throats and medical science complement each other and are not in competition. The one God is the source of both.

On Feb. 3, worshipers may receive the blessing of St. Blase given by a priest, deacon, or lay minister holding two candles against the throat and saying, "Through the intercession of St. Blase, bishop and martyr, may God deliver you from every disease of the throat and from every other evil: In the name of the Father, and of the Son, and of the Holy Spirit."

Crucified or Risen Christ on the Cross?

Question: *Should a cross have an image of Christ crucified or of Christ risen on it? One of my friends says it should always be the risen Christ. What do you think of a female Christ on the Cross?*

Answer: Images of Christ dead and of Christ risen are both perfectly acceptable. How could they not be? The Church celebrates both Good Friday and Easter Sunday. Christ's death and resurrection are inseparable. Since no image can say everything at once, it is perfectly appropriate for the different aspects of the mystery of faith to be portrayed in crosses of different kinds. Crosses with the dead Christ assume the resurrection, and crosses with Christ risen assume Good Friday. A good artist can handle both themes together. For instance, a very beautiful cross with a dead Christ prefigures the resurrection. A risen Christ with wounded hands and feet recalls Good Friday.

Regarding a female Christ on the Cross, the idea is unusual, to be sure. Edwina Sandys' famous "Christa" — which portrays Christ on the Cross as a woman — stirred up lots of controversy some years ago. If the point is to radically remake Christianity according to one's own imagination, then there's a big problem here. If the intention is to say that Christ suffers as much in women as men, then some artistic license is hardly objectionable.

The use of female Christ figures has to be approached with care, so that the true identity of the historic Jesus is respected. Given the dangers of misunderstanding and confusion, a female Christ figure on the Cross would not, in my opinion, be acceptable as a permanent or principal fixture in a church building.

Adoring the Crucifix

Question: *I've always been told that adoration is the form of worship reserved for God alone. I can understand the adoration of the Blessed Sacrament, since it is truly Christ. But isn't adoration of a crucifix idolatry?*

Answer: Adoration is indeed reserved for God alone. The act of adoration, if accorded a creature or object, would certainly be idolatry. For Mary, the angels, and saints, as well as for religious objects, the correct general term is "veneration." Occasionally the words "adoration" and "veneration" are used interchangeably, but, whatever the language invoked, Catholic commonsense intuitively knows the difference.

When the language of "adoration" is used of the Cross, Catholics are aware that they are adoring not the Cross in itself, but Christ's saving redemption wrought upon the Cross. The cross or crucifix has no meaning apart from Christ's passion, death, and resurrection.

The liturgy of Good Friday is instructive here. It contains a "Veneration of the Cross." The priest or deacon proclaims: "This is the wood of the Cross, on which hung the Savior of the world." All respond: "Come, let us worship." Lest there be any doubt about what is worshiped, the antiphon provided for the veneration itself offers clarity: "We worship you, Lord, we venerate your Cross." The acclamation popularly used for the Stations of the Cross is also telling: "We adore you, O Christ, and we bless you, because by your holy cross you have redeemed the world."

Catholics are sometimes accused of idolatry by other Christians. It is important not to let misconceptions set the terms of discussion. The use of material things in Catholic worship may be problematic for others, but Catholics should feel no compulsion to be on the defensive. What is required is an ability to explain Catholic liturgical and devotional practices intelligently and confidently.

Fish Symbol

Question: *Can you explain the origin of the fish as a Christian symbol? Why do people put it on the outside of their cars?*

Answer: The fish appeared as a symbol of Christ very early in Christianity, certainly well before by the fifth century. The Greek word for fish is "*ichthus*," which contains the first letters of the words *Iesous, CHristos, THeou, Uios, Soter*: Jesus Christ, Son of God, Savior.

The fish symbol is also associated naturally with the apostles Simon (Peter) and his brother Andrew, themselves fishermen, whom Christ called to be "fishers of men" (Mk 1:17). In early Christian preaching, Christian believers were called "little fish," since they swam spiritually in the waters of baptism.

People who wish to state their Christian allegiance publicly sometimes put the fish symbol on their cars. Call me a snob, but I am not a fan of car art, religious or otherwise. There is a certain "in your face" quality to it. (Besides, people's aggressive driving habits often conflict with the messages their car espouse externally. Recently, I saw someone with a "God is Love" sticker shout at a bicyclist at a traffic light.) Having religious or other emblems inside one's car is a different matter. The intended audience here is the driver and the passengers, not the total stranger in the car behind.

Public Processions

Question: *Our parish has Palm Sunday and Corpus Christi processions on the public street. Recently a city council member said they were illegal and that we needed a permit. What is your opinion?*

Answer: It doesn't sound like your city council member is too concerned about courting the Catholic vote! I can only speak here in generalities (a device I happen to like) because local laws vary widely on the matter of public processions, marches, and demonstrations.

It will not be news to anyone that the practice of religion has generally free rein in the U.S. (unless you do things like ritually slaughtering sheep and the health department hears about it).

However, it is reasonable that local governments ask churches and religious organizations not to cause chaos and tie up traffic by holding unannounced public processions. Generally, permits are required. The benefit to the church is that police are generally assigned to facilitate processions.

A short procession on a sidewalk around a church is in a grey area. If it is not disruptive, the police probably won't show up and shut it down. Unless your city council member is really on a roll!

Strict Christ

Question: *The large picture of Christ behind the altar at the National Shrine of the Immaculate Conception in Washington is very stern and fearsome. Why is that? Should not Christ look kind and gentle?*

Answer: The representation of Christ in the National Shrine of the Immaculate Conception is, undoubtedly, on the stern side. It belongs to a particular mode of portraying Christ that has its origin in Greek Christianity. This Christ is called the "Pantocrator," meaning the ruler of heaven and earth.

The Pantocrator Christ is not meant to strike the fear of God into faithful Christian hearts. Rather it serves to portray Christ's vanquishing power over all that is sinful, destructive, and oppressive in human history. The Pantocrator looks sternly at whatever is opposed to God's Kingdom and displays a divine power that is fearsome to the forces of evil. The image of the Pantocrator Christ may be interpreted by reference to words from the first letter of Paul to the Corinthians, which says of Christ: "Then comes the end, when he delivers the kingdom to God the Father after destroying every rule and every authority and power. For he must reign until he has put all his enemies under his feet. The last enemy to be destroyed is death. 'For God has put all things in subjection under his feet' " (1 Cor 15:24-27).

Icons

Question: *Please explain why icons are such a "big deal" these days. A pastor in a neighboring diocese has filled the church with them, and he incenses them at Mass.*

Answer: An icon is a sacred image of Eastern Christianity (Catholic or Orthodox). It is usually painted on wood, is highly stylized, and often contains rich symbolic features. The icon of the saint of the day or of a feast of Christ is often accorded particular attention. Icons of Christ and Mary are reverenced with particular devotion by being incensed and carried in solemn processions.

If the church you have in mind is an Eastern Catholic

one, then your pastor's practices are unobjectionable. However, a lot of dabbling with icons is going on in the Western churches these days. There is no protocol for the incensation of icons in the Roman liturgy.

Icons are a "big deal" because of the profound theology that accompanies them. In Eastern churches icons are not regarded as mere artistic representations, but as actually making present the mysteries of faith or the personages portrayed. Latin Catholics have much to learn from Eastern Christianity in this regard.

Gargoyles

Question: *On a radio station recently someone said that all Catholic churches are supposed to have gargoyles because Catholicism is secretly the church of the devil. What is the true story?*

Answer: If Catholicism is secretly the church of the devil, the secret has certainly been well kept, because in my 25 years as a priest, I have never been invited to participate in devil worship.

No requirement exists that all Catholic churches have gargoyles. Tell me the last time you saw a gargoyle!

As the only expert in the State of Utah on gargoyles (since our cathedral has the only ones within a radius of 1500 miles), here's what I know. Medieval churches were often built with spouts to keep the rain from running down towers and spires, causing erosion. Since these spouts didn't look very pretty, they were eventually stylized to take the shape of a mythical animal called the "gargoyle" (a combination of a cat, dog and bird — like something you might see on "The Muppets").

Eventually the erosion-preventing function of gargoyle

spouts became redundant and gargoyles became decorations. Gargoyles were then interpreted to symbolize the church's desire to keep evil at bay — a perfectly Christian objective, I would say. Any meanings beyond that tend to drift into the realm of the weird.

Holy Water

Question: *In our RCIA class, we were told that holy water has been abolished and now there is only baptismal water. Is this correct?*

Answer: Your informant has an excessively dramatic outlook on life. Though perhaps not often thought of in such terms, holy water has always been fundamentally baptismal water. Generic holy water (if you'll pardon the expression) derives its meaning from baptism.

Holy water has traditionally been used to conform Christians more closely to Christ, to sanctify things and places for the service of God and His people, and to invoke God's power against evil. All these usages are fundamentally connected to baptism.

Holy water, as Catholics understand and use it, has not been "abolished." It has, however, in recent times been more consciously associated with baptism.

Scapulars

Question: *Are scapulars still in vogue? I have not seen one in years. I heard they were abolished. Is that true?*

Answer: Scapulars are surely not in vogue these days. They have not, however, been abolished. They continue to have a valid place in Catholic devotional life.

Scapulars originated in the Middle Ages as long, narrow

pieces of cloth about shoulder width hanging to the wearer's feet on the back and the front. Trappist and Cistercian scapulars are readily identifiable as they are made of black material worn over a white tunic.

Originally scapulars were work garments meant to protect the tunic. Over time they began to assume the symbolic meaning of taking upon oneself the way of life represented by a particular religious order.

Eventually lay versions of the scapular appeared and were worn by members of third orders and confraternities. By the early twentieth century, the smaller lay scapulars usually took the forms of two small pieces of cloth bearing a religious image worn back and front over the neck.

Scapulars provide a means of dedicating oneself to a particular spirituality (Benedictine or Dominican, for instance), a way of dedicating one's daily work to God, and a reminder that to be a true disciple is, as St. Paul states, to be clothed in Christian virtue (see Col 3:12).

Blessing Candles

Question: *Does the Church still bless candles for the faithful on Candlemas Day? Are candles used for Mass blessed nowadays?*

Answer: The blessing of candles remains a part of the liturgy of Candlemas Day — officially known as the Feast of the Presentation of the Lord (February 2). A blessing of candles, possibly in the context of a procession of the people, is prescribed in the liturgy for that occasion. In some places, it is the custom to bless a supply of candles for use in the liturgy throughout the year. People may also bring their own candles to be blessed.

Additionally, a Blessing of Articles for Liturgical Use is

provided in the official Book of Blessings, which also supplies Blessings of Articles Meant to Foster the Devotion of the Christian People. These may be used at various times for the blessing of candles.

Your question raises the matter of the meaning of a blessing. Essentially, to bless something means to set it aside for sacred use. In this respect, the very act of using candles in the liturgy is itself the source of their holiness.

As a priest, I am often asked to bless Bibles. I always oblige, but never without pointing out that the Bible is intrinsically a blessed object. As the written Word of God how could it not be? In the absence of a formal blessing, objects for personal religious use are, in a certain sense, blessed automatically by their use.

Disposal of Blessed Articles

Question: *Are there rules dealing with the disposal of religious articles like rosaries and holy cards? If not, do you have any advice?*

Answer: The Church has no official guidelines for the disposal of religious articles such as those you mention. The Code of Canon Law states generally: "Sacred things which are destined for divine worship through dedication or a blessing are to be treated with reverence and not be employed for improper or profane use even if they are under the control of private individuals" (Canon 1171).

The Church does, of course, have specific norms for the disposal of eucharistic particles (they are washed into a "sacrarium," a special sink that goes directly into the earth). Traditionally other blessed objects, such as holy oils, were burned. These practices can provide some inspiration for the disposal of all religious objects. It seems appropriate that, if possible, such articles be burned or buried.

In a consumer society, we do well to avoid the "garbage disposal" mentality. The careful disposal of even the simplest religious object reminds us that the created world is God's handiwork and deserves reverence.

Superstition

Question: *My lapsed Catholic son said he was put off the Church principally by all the superstition of "little old ladies" in the Church before Vatican II. How can I answer him?*

Answer: I was raised before Vatican II (living at one point in a very rural, traditional parish in the West of Ireland overrun with "little old ladies") and I recall very little heavy-duty superstition.

Assertions about pre-Vatican II superstition in Catholicism are highly exaggerated. Superstition is the mindset that expects automatic and semi-magical results from actions that have no intrinsic relationship to the results: burying eggs in your backyard to cause harm to a neighbor; sticking pins in a doll representing your mother-in-law in the hope that she will, well, not have a good day.

Performing highly organized rituals is not necessarily superstition. It may look to the observer that "little old ladies" lighting candles, praying vociferously before statues, and expressing themselves in vigorous gestures are being superstitious. But if you were to describe superstition to them and then asked them if that's what they are doing, they would look twice at you and think you a poor, naïve soul.

Tell your son not to be so "judgmental" and closed-minded. And tell him to watch his mouth about "little old ladies." Do all this very nicely, of course.

Sacred Heart

Question: *Could you please explain the meaning of "The Sacred Heart of Jesus" and the devotion that goes with it.*

Answer: Devotion to the Sacred Heart focuses strongly on the love and mercy of Christ. The devotion arose in the twelfth century and was promoted primarily through the writings of mystics such as St. Mechtilde of Magdeburg and St. Catherine of Siena. The emphasis on the love of Christ served to counter theologies of Christ that dwelt excessively on divine judgment and punishment.

The seventeenth century witnessed a marked popularization of the devotion. St. Margaret Mary Alacoque experienced visions of the Sacred Heart at Paray-le-Monial in France and received a set of twelve promises that exerted thereafter a profound influence on popular Catholic spirituality. Official liturgical observance of the feast of the Sacred Heart was authorized in 1765. Nowadays, it is celebrated as a solemnity on the Friday of the second week after Pentecost.

First Fridays

Question: *Our family always believed that if we made the nine First Fridays none of us would die without a priest present. Recently my mother died without a priest. We are upset and confused by this. Please explain.*

Answer: The promise regarding First Fridays is the best-known element of the visions of St. Margaret Mary Alacoque, a Visitandine nun of the convent at Paray-le-Monial, France, who died in 1690.

The following is the promise which you probably have in mind: "I promise you in the excessive mercy of my Heart that my all-powerful love will grant to all those who communicate on the first Friday in nine consecutive months the grace of final penitence; they shall not die in my disgrace without receiving the sacraments; my divine Heart shall be their safe refuge in this last moment."

Visions are not doctrinal definitions in which every word and phrase has precise and exact meaning. They are more like dreams, full of symbolic language to be interpreted as a whole.

How should one understand the First Friday promise? It is fundamentally a statement that those willing to commit themselves to regular communion and devotion to the Sacred Heart of Jesus will never lack God's love and will have it when they most need it: at the time of death. There is nothing magical about the First Friday formula and it should never be interpreted as a short-cut to salvation.

Your mother may have died without a priest being physically present (a matter not actually mentioned in the famous Promise), but if she loved God and sought his will she surely did not die without the presence of the great high priest: Christ himself.

Seven Sorrows

Question: *My mother used to have great devotion to the Seven Dolors of Mary. I would like to know more about this. Is the devotion still in fashion?*

Answer: "Dolor" means "pain" or "sorrow." The devotion here refers to the seven sorrows of Mary: the prophecy of Simeon (Luke 2:34-35); the flight into Egypt (Matthew 2:13-21); the three-day search for Jesus in Jerusalem (Luke 2:41-50); and four events having to do with Jesus' suffering and death: Mary's meeting Jesus on the way to Calvary; the

Crucifixion; the taking down of Jesus' body from the Cross; and the burial in the tomb. In the current Roman calendar, a feast on this theme is observed on September 15 under the name "Our Lady of Sorrows."

The devotion might not be in fashion today, which is hardly grounds for dismissing it. (Bridesmaids' dresses in black are in fashion; baggy teenage pants are in fashion.)

The Seven Dolors devotion is certainly authentic in that it is biblically based. The devotion is a source of comfort to suffering Christians (often mothers facing difficult situations with their children) and it has more than ample relevance to those areas of the Church experiencing persecution, deprivation, or dissension.

Was Veronica Dropped from the Stations of the Cross?

Question: *In our parish, the new Stations of the Cross have dropped Veronica wiping the face of Jesus. Why is that?*

Answer: I can only guess that the reason may be that the account of Veronica wiping Jesus' face on the way to Calvary is found not in the Scriptures but in Christian legend. Only in the Middle Ages did the story of Veronica become widely popular.

However, legends are not to be dismissed too easily in Christian piety. Many families have edifying legends that pass from generation to generation. While they may not be historically founded, legends can transmit noble ideals and virtues.

The same is true of the Christian family. In a certain sense, the legend of Veronica is a pictorial reminder of the call to all Christians to act with compassion whenever they encounter the suffering Christ in their brothers and sisters. Veronica is each one of us.

The Chicken Or the Egg?

Question: *What is forbidden by the laws of abstinence from meat during Lent? I thought fried eggs were not allowed because they are chickens and therefore meat.*

Answer: Certainly eggs with identifiable chickens inside them are forbidden by the laws of abstinence from meat. I expect that anyone who even had such an experience would go off both eggs and chicken for life!

The laws of abstinence from meat (which in the United States apply on Ash Wednesday and the Fridays of Lent) forbid the eating of meat of warm-blooded animals, but not eggs (except in the unlikely case mentioned above!), milk products, or condiments of any kind, even though made of animal fat. Soups and seasonings which contain meat products are allowed. Cold-blooded animal meats including fish and frogs (should you have French tastes) are allowed.

The spirit of the law of abstinence (coupled with the fasting that goes with it) is probably not well served by substituting Australian lobster for a bologna sandwich.

Holy Saturday Spirituality

Question: *I never know what to do spiritually on Holy Saturday. The day seems empty, and I miss morning Mass on that day. Any suggestions?*

Answer: I wish more Catholics felt like you do. Holy Saturday is deliberately a spiritually empty day. Participating in the Easter Vigil (the highlight of the liturgical year) is, of course, most highly recommended. The day could also well be spent in quiet reflection. Other suggestions are: going to confession; participating in morning prayer —which every parish worth its salt celebrates on that day (I can safely say that, since our parish does it!); and fasting — which the Vatican II Constitution on the Sacred Liturgy recommended for that day (no. 110).

Going back to the spiritual emptiness of the day, the Office of Readings for Holy Saturday offers a moving passage from an ancient homily establishing the theme of the day: "Something strange is happening — there is a great silence on earth today, a great silence and stillness. The whole earth keeps silence because the King is asleep. The earth trembled and is still because God has fallen asleep in the flesh and he has raised up all who have slept ever since the world began. God has died in the flesh and hell trembles with fear. He has gone to search for our first parent, as for a lost sheep. Greatly desiring to visit those who live in darkness and in the shadow of death, he has gone to free from sorrow the captives Adam and Eve, he who is both God and the son of Eve."

May as Easter or Month of Mary

Question: *Our parish liturgy committee told our Altar Society that we could not build a Mary shrine in the church this May as that month is part of the Easter season and Easter overrules Marian devotion. Is this correct?*

Answer: I've always found Altar Societies to be formidable outfits. Hopefully yours did not take the decree lying down. (And where was the pastor in all this?)

In authentic Catholic devotion, Mary is always depicted and celebrated in her relationship to her Son. She is venerated during Easter not in or for herself, but as mother of the Church rejoicing over Jesus' resurrection. The Mary of May is therefore the Mary of Easter.

The figure of Mary rejoicing at the Lord's resurrection is beautifully captured in the *"Regina Coeli,"* the ancient antiphon for the Easter season: "Queen of Heaven, rejoice, alleluia. The Son whom you merited to bear, alleluia, has risen as he said, alleluia: Rejoice and be glad, O Virgin Mary, alleluia! For the Lord has truly risen, alleluia."

We read in the Acts of the Apostles that after Jesus' ascension, the apostles "devoted themselves to prayer together with the women and Mary the mother of Jesus" (1:14).

Traditional Catholic depictions of Pentecost find Mary with the Apostles as the Spirit of the risen Christ descends upon them.

There need be no opposition between May devotion to Mary and the Easter season. Indeed, each enriches the other. Your parish liturgy committee might need to lighten up a little.

Infant of Prague

Question: *Our parish church has a beautiful Infant of Prague with lovely robes for each season. The pastor wants to get rid of it because he says this devotion is "outdated and silly." Where did this devotion come from?*

Answer: I've seen statues of the Infant of Prague that are excessively glitzy — one, in particular, whose elaborate robes reminded me of Elvis Presley. Statuary in churches should be of good artistic quality, be well integrated into the whole liturgical scheme, not have excessive prominence, and not encourage exaggerated devotion.

However, the presence of an image of the Infant of Prague in a church and devotion to it are not in themselves outdated or silly, since the object of devotion is Christ himself.

Devotion to the Infant of Prague began about the middle of the seventeenth century in the Carmelite community in Prague in the present-day Czech Republic. The benefactor who gave the image to the Carmelites did so with these words:

"As long as you honor this image, you shall never want." This devotion spread all over the world, and the Infant of Prague has become a popular focus of prayer especially in times of spiritual or material poverty. That's pretty basic Christianity in operation, I'd say!

Irish Purgatory

Question: *I have heard of St. Patrick's Purgatory in Ireland. What is it about and is it still functioning today?*

Answer: St. Patrick's Purgatory is an ancient pilgrimage site located on the island of Lough Derg in County Donegal. In the Middle Ages, a church and a man-made cave were constructed on the island as a result of a legend that a certain Sir Owain, a knight of King Stephen's court, descended for his sins into purgatory on an Irish island.

According to the legend, an earthly purgatory was set up by St. Patrick, who would take sinners to this purgatory-on-earth to see the pain and suffering of the souls of the departed in the hope of bringing about repentance and reparation.

St. Patrick's Purgatory remains today a popular place of pilgrimage. It involves a three-day retreat, with fasting, minimal sleep, Mass, and confession. Lough Derg is not recommended to the faint-hearted or those of delicate constitution. All in all, it's a pretty rigorous and daunting place.

Our Lady of Knock

Question: *My mother was from Knock in Ireland. I know Mary appeared there, but I don't know much more. Was there a message that she delivered?*

Answer: Ireland's national Marian shrine in the town of Knock in County Mayo dates from August 21, 1879. On that day, the figures of Mary, Joseph, and John the Apostle appeared enveloped in light on the outside of the village church. In the vision, an altar also appeared with a cross and Lamb upon it. The apparition was repeated twice in 1880.

Stories of miracles brought hundreds to the town. Fifteen solid citizens positively testified that what they saw was not an illusion. After an inquiry, church authorities accepted the testimony, declaring that the apparitions were "trustworthy and satisfactory."

There was no explicit message at Knock, only a comforting and uplifting vision in a cold, rainy, windy, gray, barren, desolate, dreary village to a people who were forlorn and poor in body and spirit. Someone once said, "The message of Knock is: if Mary could appear there, she can appear anywhere." Of course, I would never say that, but the point is not completely frivolous.

Tomb of Mary Magdalene

Question: *During a recent trip to France, I came across the Shrine of St. Mary Magdalene in the village of Saint-Maximin. I was told Mary Magdalene is buried there, but my pastor told me this is nonsense. Which is correct?*

Answer: According to the "Life of Saint Mary Magdalene" written by Rabanus Maurus in the ninth century, Mary Magdalene went to France, lived in a cave in the hills of La Sainte-Baum, and was buried in the village of Saint-Maximin. Numerous popes, and in particular Boniface VIII (1294-1303), granted indulgences to those who visited the tomb in Saint-Maximin. Many saints, including St. Catherine of Siena, St. Vincent de Paul and St. Bridget of Sweden came to venerate at the grotto of Saint-Maximin.

No historically verifiable data supports the belief that

Mary Magdalene is buried at Saint-Maximin. The absence of strict historical evidence does not, however, mean that the claim is disproved. This belief belongs in the category of Christian legend — stories that may be true, but are not historically verifiable. Legends are akin to family histories transmitted from generation to generation. Many of us have stories about our grandparents or great-grandparents that have no record other than family memory.

Certain legends are, of course, intrinsically silly, and we should be careful about gullibility, especially in matters of faith. But the fact is, Mary Magdalene is buried somewhere! The tomb in Saint-Maximin is venerated "as if" she were buried there. Like all the saints, Mary Magdalene is present wherever the Eucharist is celebrated. She is certainly present and may be invoked in a special way in the grotto of Saint-Maximin, hallowed by 1,000 years of devotion.

The Shroud of Turin

Question: *If the Shroud of Turin is proved to be a fake, wouldn't that undermine the credibility of the Church?*

Answer: Had the Church ever declared itself authoritatively and decisively in favor of the authenticity of the Shroud of Turin, it certainly would. But the Church has not done so and would not do so. The Church in Italy recognizes the Shroud as worthy of veneration because it brings home to people in a realistic way the truth of Christ's suffering and death and encourages devotion to the mystery of Christ's passion and resurrection.

Ecclesiastical authorities have allowed various scientific tests on the Shroud. Whether these will prove anything one way or the other in the long run is not of ultimate importance.

I remember the answer Cardinal Ballestrero of Turin

gave to a prominent U.S. news reporter studying the Shroud some years ago. The reporter asked: "Your Eminence, what if the Shroud is proven to be only from the middle ages?" To which the cardinal replied: "It wouldn't matter; our interest in the Shroud is spiritual, not scientific" (or words to that effect). A good answer!

The Shroud is a venerable heirloom of the Church, and it is venerated "as if" it were the burial cloth of Christ. Such an approach is incomprehensible to the rationalistic mind, but is perfectly consistent with Catholic spiritual and devotional life.

Footprints of Christ

Question: *When I was in Rome last year, I saw the supposed footmarks of Christ in a church on the Appian Way. The tour guide said they are historically authentic. What do you think?*

Answer: According to a legend found in the "Acts of Peter" (an apocryphal book not found in the Bible), Peter was persuaded to leave Rome during the persecution of Nero to escape martyrdom. On the outskirts of the city, he met Christ carrying the Cross. When Peter asked him where he was going, Christ replied, "To Rome, to be crucified again." Whereupon Peter, stricken with shame, returned to Rome and his own martyrdom. The Church of Santa Maria in Palmis on the Appian Way is said to mark the spot and is known as the *Domine Quo Vadis* Church (from the Latin words, "Lord, where are you going?"). The church contains what is regarded as a reproduction of the footprints of Christ.

Your tour guide was overextending him- or herself by claiming that the footmarks in the Appian Way church are "historically authentic." Should they then be discounted? No.

They are reminders that Christ did indeed walk the earth (and did have real footprints). Artifacts of the kind you mention bring home to us the historical reality of Christ and surely represent something of the real struggle of Peter facing martyrdom.

Home Schooling

Question: *My daughter and her husband home-school their children. They are a wonderful family, but they get a hard time from their parish for this. Why are pastors and religious education directors suspicious of home schooling?*

Answer: Probably because pastors and parish directors of education do not know much about home schooling. Home schoolers are unfairly associated with right-wing movements of various sorts. Furthermore, pastors and their education staff sometimes think that home schoolers don't trust Catholic religious education. (Sadly, there can occasionally exist some grounds for mistrust.)

Since the Church regards parents as the primary educators of their children, home schooling is, in principle, an acceptable approach to the formation of children. The challenge is to ensure that the quality of home schooling is strong and that children are adequately socialized. Parents wisely seek guidance from and interact with home-school resource organizations and networks.

Recently, the Diocese of Pittsburgh released a document entitled "Faith Education in the Home: Catholic Homeschooling," which offers guidelines and support for homeschooling families. I have not seen the publication, but people whose judgment I trust speak positively of it.

To resolve the problem you mention, my recommendation is that home-school families should go out of their way to be as cooperative with — and as involved as possible in — their parish communities.

Faith Healers

Question: *My sister wants to go to Ireland to see a faith healer to take away the pain in her back. I think she is being downright silly. What is the Church's position on this?*

Answer: While the Church is all for getting rid of back pain and has no position on going to Ireland, pastoral wisdom would offer a caution on going near Irish faith healers. A faith healer is a person who is thought to have unusual powers of healing.

There are, of course, a great variety of faith healers ranging from persons of genuine piety, prudence, and faith to the wackiest and the daftest. The only one I ever knew in Ireland was a woman who all year round wore two plastic coats tied with a rope. She rode a man's bicycle and drank a lot (both at the same time).

On the other hand, faith healing is an important feature of the modern charismatic movement and it has been associated with saintly and modest figures over the centuries. Fundamentally, genuine faith healing is faith-filled prayer for the sick. In its positive expressions, it is clearly God's work.

Faith healing works in a wide variety of ways. Some reported instances of faith healing may be explained by the power of suggestion. Faith healers are attuned to the close relationship between mind and body. They recognize that positive thinking has physical benefits.

Your sister would be well advised to think twice about going to Ireland (or anywhere else) to see a faith healer. She would do well at least to find out the name of a priest in whose parish the faith healer resides and seek his advice before calling Aer Lingus.

Focolare Movement

Question: *I recently heard about the Focolare Movement. Please explain where it came from and what is its purpose.*

Answer: *Focolare* (meaning hearth or fireside) is a movement of spiritual renewal that began in Trent, Italy, in 1943 under the leadership of Chiara Lubich. The spirituality of the movement is based on the promise of Jesus that "Where two or three are gathered in my name, there am I in the midst of them" (Mt 18:20). Jesus' prayer "that all may be one" (see Jn 17:21) also holds a high importance in the movement, which seeks consciously to create unity among Christians, as well as others.

Originally an association of virgins devoted to the Virgin Mary, the movement now includes married members of both sexes. Some members live in community houses, continuing their ordinary employment. Others (especially the married) live in their own homes, but are intensely involved in community meetings and activities.

The vision of community life in the New Testament church, a strong emphasis on the Eucharist, intensive study of the word of God, and devotion to Mary remain the bases of the movement, which is now found in over sixty countries. In the U.S., Focolare groups exist in many of the major cities. Focolare spirituality has been successfully adapted for use in a number of Protestant and Anglican churches.

Human Life International

Question: *What is Human Life International? I have been on the mailing list of the organization for some time without knowing much about it. Is it in good standing in the Church?*

Answer: Human Life International was founded in 1981 by Father Paul Marx, O.S.B., a monk of St. John's Abbey,

Collegeville, Minnesota. The organization is dedicated to protecting the unborn, the elderly, and the handicapped; strengthening family life; encouraging premarital and marital chastity; and promoting the practice of natural family planning. The organization conducts its work through research, education, and service projects, and it makes available information on medical-moral issues relating to human life.

The aims of Human Life International are unimpeachable and crucial to the development of Catholic family life and sexual morality. There are some who think the organization occasionally errs through a lack of prudence and charity in its public actions and postures. However, I have heard nobody seriously suggest that the organization is not in good standing in the Church. Indeed, many church leaders regard it very highly.

Legion of Mary

Question: *I have been an active member of the Legion of Mary for over 30 years. It is a very effective organization because of the work it does. I cannot understand why it is not emphasized more in our parishes. Your comments, please.*

Answer: The Legion of Mary is one of the many excellent lay Catholic organizations that were operative well before Vatican II. It belongs to that category of activities called the "lay apostolate," that is, organizations that are lay- (rather than clergy-) led and focused on the lay role in society at large (rather than on work "within" the Church).

An unintended consequence of Vatican II was that as lay roles in the church were opened up, lay activity in the social arena began to wane somewhat. The laity became, some would say, clericalized after Vatican II, so that the "active" Catholic today is seen as the reader, the eucharistic minister, the altar assistant, the religious education teacher and not so much the Catholic parent, professional, or worker committed to Christian service in "the world" — often through lay organizations.

The Legion of Mary does not need to look for its vision and vitality to clergy leadership, but to lay talent. It is up to members of the Legion of Mary and similar organizations to renew their leadership energies and goals from within. If pastors are not interested, I suggest that Legionaries forge ahead on their own, as long as they stay within the regulations of the organization.

Cursillo Movement

Question: *My in-laws are big into the Cursillo Movement. What does it mean and where did it come from? Why do so many movements like this exist in the Church?*

Answer: The Cursillo Movement originated in Spain in 1949 as a program of organized renewal devised by a group of laymen, with the assistance of Bishop Hervas y Benet of Mallorca. The term *cursillo* means "little course." The program follows three stages, each consisting of three days: preparation ("precursilllo"), the course proper ("cursillo"), and the follow-up ("post-cursillo").

The purpose of the cursillo process is to transform society by changing the hearts, minds, and lives of Christians. The cursillo proper involves an intensive weekend built around fifteen talks, of which ten are given by laymen. Living together as a Christian community is an important feature of the weekend.

Those who have participated in the movement are called "cursillistas." They meet on a regular basis after the initial program in what is called the "ultreya," the small group. The

Spiritual Exercises of St. Ignatius Loyola play an important part in cursillo devotion.

Why do so many such movements exist? Because the Holy Spirit inspires countless means to help individuals and communities follow the way of Christ in the diverse and ever-changing circumstances of human society.

Benedictine Oblates

Question: *What is a Benedictine Oblate? One in our parish wears a full habit, and everyone thinks she is a nun. I am confused.*

Answer: The title "Benedictine Oblate" is used today to refer to lay men and women living "in the world" (in the married or single state) who join themselves spiritually to a particular Benedictine community and seek to observe in the particular circumstances of their lives some aspects of the Rule of St. Benedict.

Originally, Benedictine oblates lived around and cultivated the lands owned by monasteries. They participated in Mass and the Liturgy of the Hours and wore a simplified form of the order's habit.

Benedictine oblates may be buried in the habit of the order (a somewhat ambiguous matter nowadays, since some Benedictine communities do not wear habits).

I know of no protocol for Benedictine oblates wearing the habit outside of monasteries. The "nun" in your parish wearing a full habit is, I suspect, a free-lancer. Your confusion is justified.

Vatican Newspaper

Question: *As a new Catholic, I know that the Vatican publishes a daily newspaper. What is it, and where can I get it?*

Answer: The daily newspaper of the Holy See is called *L'Osservatore Romano*, founded in 1861 under the leadership of Catholic laymen. Pope Leo XIII purchased the newspaper in 1890. Since then it has been referred to as the "official newspaper of the pope." The paper covers international news, publishes papal speeches and homilies, and announces the official initiatives of the Holy See.

The daily edition is in Italian; so you will want to be sure that your reading ability in Italian is respectable before usefully ordering it. However, weekly editions are printed in English, French, Spanish, Portuguese, German, and Polish. The weekly English edition may be ordered from: The Cathedral Foundation, *L'Osservatore Romano*—English Edition, P.O. Box 777, Baltimore, MD 21203.

Index of Forbidden Books

Question: *What is the Index of Forbidden Books? Does it still exist? If not, why not?*

Answer: The Index of Forbidden Books was an official list of writings that Catholics were formerly forbidden to read or possess. Permission to read a book placed on the Index had to be obtained from the Holy See through the Holy Office. Persons who wrote, published, read, or kept forbidden books were subject to automatic excommunication.

The Index was first drawn up by the Congregation of the Inquisition under Pope Paul IV in 1557. In 1571, Pope Pius V established a special Congregation of the Index, which was responsible for maintaining and revising the list of prohibited books. The Congregation of the Index survived until 1917, when its responsibilities were transferred to the Holy Office, today called the Congregation for the Doctrine of the Faith. In 1966, the

Index and its attendant excommunications were abolished.

Why did the Church drop the Index? First, it was occasionally the source of abuse and ecclesiastical politicking. Second, it seemed offensive to the more open atmosphere regarding theological thought that came after Vatican II. Third, in the modern age when people have easy access to books and censorship has less effect, placing books on a forbidden Index would only generate stronger interest. More than one theological author in recent decades has expressed a desire to be placed on the Index of Forbidden Books, on the grounds that this would provide the greatest publicity possible and hike his or her book into the best-seller list!

Best Catholic Reading

Question: *What is the best newspaper or magazine for a Catholic like myself to keep up on the life of the Church? I am not an intellectual or scholar.*

Answer: Why, *Our Sunday Visitor*, of course! Actually, I do mean that. *Our Sunday Visitor* is, in my opinion, the best national Catholic paper available these days. (It's not that *Our Sunday Visitor* is good merely because I write for it. I write for it because it's good!) It's substantive, interesting, balanced and — not least — always charitable, lacking the "edge" that characterizes some other publications to the right and the left. I would also recommend the *National Catholic Register*, *The Catholic World Report*, *Inside the Vatican*, and *Catholic Parent*. Your final choices, of course, will depend on your spiritual needs and state in life.

Mormonism and Catholicism

Question: *Can you recommend a good book on the differences between Mormonism and Catholicism?*

Answer: There is a real dearth of adequate material on this matter. What does exist often caricatures or distorts either Catholic or Mormon belief and practice.

The best popular text of which I am aware is written by Father William Taylor, an Idaho priest "with Mormon roots." The book is entitled *A Tale of Two Cities: A Comparison Between the Mormon and the Catholic Religious Experiences*.

The book is available from Little Red Hen Publishing, Pocatello, Idaho (208-233-3755). Father Taylor's treatment of Mormonism seeks to be accurate, fair, and charitable.

Imitation of Christ

Question: *Recently my mother left me a book called* The Imitation of Christ. *Someone told me it's ancient and out of date, and that I shouldn't read it. What is your advice?*

Answer: Lots of things are ancient, meaning "around a long time" (God, the Church, the Bible, heaven), but that hardly means that they are out of date. There is nothing so tired and outdated as some of the spiritual writings published in the past thirty years (I'll be nice and not mention books or authors — to your disappointment, I'm sure). At the same time, ancient classics remain perennially fresh.

The Imitation of Christ is a devotional book, published anonymously in 1418 but now attributed to Thomas à Kempis, a Dutch priest. Sometimes called "The Following of Christ," it offers a way of Christian perfection.

Written in a popular style, the work is divided into four parts: practical advice about the spiritual life; intensive living of the interior life; inward consolation; and devotion to the Blessed Sacrament.

The basic theme of the book is that, since Jesus Christ is

truly divine and truly human, by imitating Christ the Christian becomes more like Christ. Does that sound old-fashioned or out of date to you?

Next to the Bible, *The Imitation of Christ* is the most widely read spiritual book in the world.

My advice? Read it.

Reading Cardinal Newman

Question: *For someone who is a beginner and wants to become familiar with the writings of Cardinal Newman, what do you recommend?*

Answer: Because of his Victorian writing style and complex prose, some people think that Cardinal Newman is not the easiest person to read. However, many believe that his most beautiful and spiritually uplifting writings are his homilies. The collection entitled "Parochial and Plain Sermons" is not the place to start, but it represents some of the most profound and lovely writings in Christian literature. If I were stranded on a desert island for the rest of my life with one volume for spiritual reading, this would be it!

For the beginner, I recommend two books. The first is by A.N. Wilson and is entitled *John Henry Newman: Prayers, Poems, Meditations*. The volume provides short and very readable extracts from Newman for every day of the year. The second, edited by Jules M. Brady, S.J., and entitled *Newman for Everyone*, arranges short passages from Newman under the heading "101 Questions Answered Imaginatively by Newman."

Mourning Angels

Question: *Why are the statues of angels in cemeteries often mourning and crying? I thought angels are always happy.*

Answer: If I ever get hit by a truck crossing the street, I hope my guardian angel will not disinterestedly proclaim "I'm outta here!" God cares deeply about human suffering and so do the angels and saints. Angels are depicted in Christian art in all kinds of emotional states. They are not represented as joyful in pictures of the crucifixion and other sorrowful scenes in the lives of Christ, Mary, and the martyrs. They are generally in such situations depicted hiding their faces, wringing their hands, and manifesting intense grief. One famous representation shows a mourning angel kneeling before a crown of thorns with tears upon his face.

In cemeteries, angels are often portrayed as guardians or wardens of the bodies of the dead. They are found in many mournful poses as they grace gravestones and tombs. The cherubim are commonly found on the burial places of babies and children, expressing at once sadness and hope.

Pre-Planning Funerals

Question: *Many of my friends are pre-planning their funerals so that they will not burden their children when they die. Something makes me not want to do that, but I still don't want to be a burden. Please comment.*

Answer: Pre-planning funerals (or what some call Pay-Now-Go-Later planning) is increasingly popular in our society. It has some things to be said in its favor. First, people can be sure that there will be some resemblance between what they want and what they get for their funerals, and their funerals will not be subject to the whims (or cheapness) of less reliable children or relatives.

Second, if the next-of-kin are elderly or in ill-health, undue pressure is not placed on them by a death in the family.

Third, if the next-of-kin are far away and the question as to how and where one should be buried is unclear, then pre-planning helps.

Beyond that, I don't buy the arguments. Since death is something that "happens" to one — as is being raised from the dead — then a funeral is something that "happens" to one, too. Planning the details of your funeral (hymns, flowers, casket, wardrobe) and paying for it yourself seems to smack of an individualistic consumer culture lacking the bonds of human solidarity.

If the final chapter of your earthly life (including illness and old age), as well as your death, funeral, burial, and the closing of your estate (to put it grandly) are burdens on your children and relatives, then so be it.

The Gospel of Christ sets a high priority on care for the elderly, the dying and dead — in short, on the sharing of burdens. Being a parent, a spouse, a relative, a friend, or a neighbor has its burdensome side. Carrying burdens well is what makes life noble, virtuous, and faithful.

Talking through one's funeral with reliable children and relatives, and even giving them the cash to pay for it (if you can afford it and they can't) is eminently reasonable. But I do not recommend pre-planning funerals in detail, especially if it means dealing with a mortician —whose financial interests in the plans may be less than virtuous.

I decided long ago that if no one is around to care enough to give me a decent burial, I am not going to leave a cent behind to resolve their dilemma!

Scattering Cremains

Question: *I get the impression that scattering of the cremains is "discouraged" but not "forbidden." This seems to imply scattering is permitted. Please clarify.*

Answer: The Church "requires" that cremated remains not be scattered. That is the operative language on this matter. In the Spring of 1997, Rome approved an Appendix to the Order of Christian Funerals for the United States. No. 416 of that document states: "The cremated remains of a body should be treated with the same respect given to the human body from which they come. This includes the use of a worthy vessel to contain the ashes, the manner in which they are carried, the care and attention to appropriate placement and transport, and the final disposition. The cremated remains should be buried in a grave or entombed in a mausoleum or columbarium. The practice of scattering cremated remains on the sea, from the air, or on the ground, or keeping cremated remains in the home of a relative or friend of the deceased are not the reverent disposition that the Church requires. Whenever possible, appropriate means for recording with dignity the memory of the deceased should be adopted, such as a plaque or stone which records the name of the deceased."

The Church is powerless if after the funeral people choose to ignore Church norms on this matter. The best means of prevention is a clear presentation in parishes and dioceses — and among funeral directors — of the Church's norms and the rationale behind them.

Ashes to Mulch

Question: *Recently our son's cremated ashes were disposed of by his friends. Some of them divided up the ashes and others made flower pots out of them. The rest of the ashes were scattered all over the backyard. I know it is not allowed to bury ashes in a backyard. We could not bring ourselves to attend the ceremony, which was conducted by a priest. Were we wrong?*

Answer: First, a priest should not have been conducting a service such as you describe, since it goes against the prescribed practice of the Church.

When you say that it is "not allowed to bury ashes in a backyard," you raise an interesting question. What the church objects to is the dispersal of the ashes. As I understand matters, there is no objection to people burying ashes on family property (aristocracies have been doing this for centuries), as long as the grave is marked, blessed, and properly maintained.

Were you wrong not to attend the service you describe? Attending an event which would be unnecessarily painful for you and of which you (correctly) disapprove is above and beyond the call of duty. You can still pray for your son and perhaps have a permanent marker erected in a cemetery or mausoleum to serve as the focus of your remembrance.

Why Bury Ashes?

Question: *I believe everything the Church teaches, but do not go along with the burial of cremated ashes. In fact, in my will I have specified that they not be buried. Please comment.*

Answer: Sounds like you intend to go out fighting! Paragraph 15 of the 1969 Introduction to the Order of Funerals states: "Funeral rites are to be granted to those who have chosen cremation, unless there is evidence that their choice was dictated by anti-Christian motives."

The funeral is to be celebrated in a manner that "clearly expresses the Church's preference for the custom of burying the dead, after the example of Christ's own will to be buried." Properly, ashes are interred in a cemetery (often in an existing family plot) or placed in a niche above ground. (Many Catholic cemeteries provide these nowadays.)

Among the unapproved alternatives are having your ashes (a) left abandoned at the mortuary — surely an anti-climactic ending to one's earthly career; (b) scattered over some favorite landscape (a practice not considered ecologically sensitive these days); or (c) kept at home on the mantle piece of a relative or friend (inviting spooked commentary from house guests).

These alternatives suggest a lack of clear consciousness about the dignity of the human body or the ashes of the deceased. Even as ashes, the human body is the stuff of the Resurrection. Having one's ashes properly interred is an act of profound faith in Divine Providence.

Real Burials

Question: *In funerals we talk about "burial," yet in the U.S. the burial after the funeral is often unfinished, with the casket left on top of the grave. This seems wrong to me. Please comment.*

Answer: I'm with you on this! As long as I live, I'll never get used to the practice of leaving the casket on top of the grave and walking away.

There are a number of explanations for leaving burials unfinished nowadays. One is cultural squeamishness about death and the tendency to sanitize funerals (with fake grass and carefully hidden earth). Another is the belief that it is too traumatic for mourners to see the casket lowered into the ground — after all, family members have been known to jump in after the casket (to which I respond — based on childhood experience in the west of Ireland — I've never seen anyone jump into a grave who didn't climb out in a minute or less). A third is that grave-diggers have been replaced by bulldozers and no one wants to hang around to see the grave area turn into a construction site.

From my sporadic research, I know of no reason why funeral and cemetery directors cannot facilitate the integration of actual burials into funeral rites. The use of human grave fillers rather than machinery would solve the technical problem.

Gregorian Masses

Question: *I can't find a priest who will say Gregorian Masses. My pastor says the idea is out of date. Is this true? What can I do instead? This was an old tradition in my family.*

Answer: The tradition of Gregorian Masses involved offering on thirty consecutive days a Mass for a deceased person. Belief in the efficacy of Gregorian Masses in obtaining the release of souls from purgatory is based on a private revelation of Pope Gregory I. In 1888, the Sacred Congregation for Indulgences declared that the confidence of Catholics in such Masses is reasonable and edifying. Nevertheless, the Church is not bound by private revelations.

Gregorian Masses have fallen into disuse in recent times for a number of reasons. The practice appeared to put too much confidence in a formula (30 Masses in a row) and could give the impression that God's hands are tied, so to speak. However, the fundamental elements of a well-intentioned practice are never out of date.

I suggest that the basic idea be renewed in this way: a person actually goes to Mass for 30 days to pray for the soul of the deceased as a sign of solidarity and loving companionship.

What follows is by no means an exhaustive list. But those who wish to know more about Gregorian Masses or perhaps schedule them may write: Franciscan Missions, Inc., P.O. Box 130, Waterford, WI 53185; Franciscan Mission Associates, P.O. Box 598, Dept. M, Mount Vernon, NY 10551-0598; Pauline Fathers, P.O. Box 2049, Doylestown, PA 18901; or Aid to the Church in Need, P.O. Box 576, Deer Park, NY 11729-0576.

INDEX

Our Sunday Visitor. . .
Your Source for Discovering
the Riches of the Catholic Faith

Our Sunday Visitor has an extensive line of materials for young children, teens, and adults. Our books, Bibles, booklets, CD-ROMs, audios, and videos are available in bookstores worldwide.

To receive a FREE full-line catalog or for more information, call **Our Sunday Visitor** at **1-800-348-2440**. Or write, **Our Sunday Visitor** / 200 Noll Plaza / Huntington, IN 46750.

- -

Please send me: ___A catalog

Please send me materials on:

___Apologetics and catechetics   ___Reference works

___Prayer books   ___Heritage and the saints

___The family   ___The parish

Name_____

Address_____Apt._____

City_____State_____Zip_____

Telephone (   ) _____

A23BBABP

- -

Please send a friend: ___A catalog

Please send a friend materials on:

___Apologetics and catechetics   ___Reference works

___Prayer books   ___Heritage and the saints

___The family   ___The parish

Name_____

Address_____Apt._____

City_____State_____Zip_____

Telephone (   ) _____

A23BBABP

- -

Our Sunday Visitor
200 Noll Plaza
Huntington, IN 46750
Toll free: 1-800-348-2440
E-mail: osvbooks@osv.com
Website: www.osv.com